THE
5·2·1
PRINCIPLE

Five Processes
+
Two Questions
+
One Routine
=
Success

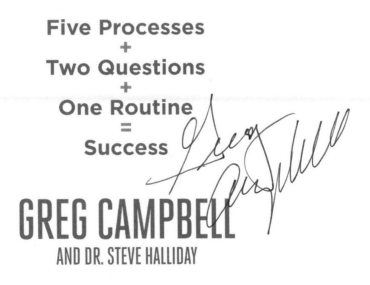

GREG CAMPBELL
AND DR. STEVE HALLIDAY

"Great use of examples and business insight. This book can easily be read in a weekend, however the concepts will cause you to rethink just about every way you do business for years to come—no matter if you're a CEO of an international company or you own the local store on Main Street."

—Hugh Siler, entrepreneur

"He is a soft spoken, very successful business man who challenges you continually with the things and decisions you know you need to make. His quiet insight into areas of your company stretch growth in both yourself and your company in a very positive way. We have put his principles to work in our company with definite proven success and growth."

—Tom Darmstandler, CEO *Kona Chips*

Contact the author at:
coilstories@gmail.com
coilstories.com

CONTENTS

ACKNOWLEDGEMENTS

Books such as this do not happen by accident but through years of interaction with hundreds if not thousands of people. Each of these interactions enriched my life in one or more ways. My life has been complete in relationships with family, work, non-profits, education and friends. Some of those stories are reflected in this little book.

There are a few people that have been particularly encouraging to me. My wife, Antje, has been consistently encouraging to me, believing in me and the ideas in this book! Without the gently "you can do it", I would not even have undertaken the task.

Tony Thomopoulos was the first to really say, "Greg, you really need to write these ideas down." Drs. Jerry Root, Tony Payne and Jeff Davis, all professors at Wheaton College have been giving advice and encouragement for years. Lastly, I'm grateful for my fellow employees that put up with my sometimes crazy ideas and for the past twenty years the individuals and organizations that I've been privileged to work with and who have all challenged my thinking and helped me grow in so many ways.

Mostly, I am grateful for Steve Halliday. He, as a professional author and writer, agreed to come alongside me and take my ideas and thoughts and make them intelligible in writing. For that I am for ever in his debt.

Becoming the Best You Possible

For the better part of three decades, the broad principles and simple questions laid out in this book have guided and fueled my leadership career. Whether the challenge concerned multi-million dollar decisions I made in my role as a principal at Coldwell Banker, or helping a young businessman to think through his career options in a very different role as a family friend, I have seen this approach consistently launch men and women from all strata of life into a healthy pattern of success.

At the core of the book lies a fierce interest in people and in their worlds, as well as a firm conviction that success in business depends as much on a genuine concern for one's colleagues as it does on sound fiscal decisions. I strongly believe that if we focus outward, we can achieve far more than if we focus inward. Learning to adopt an outward focus, coupled with a thirst for broad-based knowledge beyond one's narrow professional interests, will set up every leader to achieve at very high levels.

I don't pretend to be a John Maxwell or a Ken Blanchard, so in this sense, *The 5-2-1 Principle* is not a "typical" leadership book. Even so, I've seen this approach deliver such dependably strong results over the decades that business associates and others have long pressed me to "put something in writing." I finally did.

You can effectively apply this approach to your own situation, no matter who you are, what you do, or where you work within your organization. I know this because I've worked effectively both with young and inexperienced leaders and with older, more seasoned veterans. The principles and philosophy espoused in this book apply equally well to both groups.

My career has taught me that if we care about people, we will care about them in their totality. We will take an interest in every aspect of their lives. And when we display this kind of care in our professional pursuits—when we help our people to take care of themselves as whole persons—we set up our organizations to take big jumps in productivity. By helping the individuals around us to develop as human beings, we make it possible to turbocharge our corporate success.

The philosophy underlying *The 5-2-1 Principle* has a cyclical nature. That is, the principles and key activities described in it circle back repeatedly. By asking and answering the two core questions—"Why do we do what we do?" and "What can we do better?"—and by moving through each of the five I's, we come to see where we need to make changes. And once we finish that task, we start the process all over again. Really, it never stops. That's how we keep reaching new, exciting vistas and continue to get better, both personally and as a business.

Let me say it again: This approach is people-driven as much as it is business-driven. It's about becoming your own best self and seeing how you can make a positive difference in the lives of others. So if you're twenty years old, you can make a difference. If you're sixty-five years old, you can make a difference. The principles apply regardless.

This book is not rocket science. At root, all I'm trying to do is to help people learn how to pay attention. I get a great deal of satisfaction when I watch someone apply these principles and then hear them say, "Wow! That was an *interesting* day! I can't wait until tomorrow."

If I had to summarize this approach, I'd say it's about becoming all that we have the capacity to be. Or framed in a more personal way, we could ask a question:

How do I become the best me possible?

The overarching goal is to align who you are with who you want to be, in the context of how you're connected with others in both your professional and personal worlds. As you might guess, I doubt we ever *really* separate our lives as we imagine we do. We try to pretend that we leave home when we go to work, and we leave work when we go home. But by and large, there's very little truth to that conceit. The stress we feel at home we bring to work, and the frustrations we encounter at work we bring home. We compartmentalize the two worlds as best we can, but the separation never comes close to 100 percent.

That's why I advocate an integrated approach with intertwined steps. This book therefore outlines a whole-person philosophy that deeply affects all your worlds: business, personal, spiritual, educational. Its principles have broad application to all aspects of a leader's life, and those principles revolve around a genuine interest in others. That's at the core. If we're genuinely interested in others, then the question is, how do we appropriately utilize that interest to help us become better in what we do, both as individuals and organizations? I have very little interest in writing a book that confines itself to business leadership principles alone. I've seen too many leaders "succeed" in business while flaming out everywhere else.

So if a person can't (or more likely, won't) take the first or second step in *The 5-2-1 Principle*, I doubt there's much sense in moving to the third step. If that describes you, then frankly you're better off going somewhere else for the help you need. Formulaic approaches are a dime a dozen; pick one. But if you're ready to grow broadly curious and develop the ability to see new things, and then get intentional about your personal and professional growth, then the approach I advocate here has the power to revolutionize *everything*.

What I have to offer in *The 5-2-1 Principle* is more philosophical, more basic, more all-embracing than the norm. It probably has more in common with classic resources on servant leadership, books by authors such as Max Dupree and Robert Greenleaf, than it does with most business books published today. You won't find any "secrets" in it. But when you apply this approach—no matter who you are or where you are or what you do or how you fit into an organization—it has the muscle to set you up for success.

In all your worlds.

Why Do What We Do?

I once got a call from the leaders of a small organization that had changed its name several times in just a few years. The leaders' natural indecisiveness had led them to seek outside counsel about the future direction of their organization. They felt "under the pile" and lost about what to do.

After we spent some time getting to know one another, I asked the first of the two big questions: "Why are you doing this work? Is it about creating a legacy organization that will continue after you're gone? Or is this about something good you want to do right now, at this specific time in your life, while you're able to do it? Those are two radically different 'whys.'"

They didn't answer right away. In fact, they couldn't answer for many months. I sensed that they had avoided making a decision because they honestly didn't know what they wanted. Perhaps they hoped the question would either go away or answer itself. When it didn't, they finally saw the need to dig deep and seriously ponder the why question, regardless of where the answer might lead.

In time, they realized that their ministry was for now, at this particular time, and was not a legacy organization. Once they saw that truth and could admit it, they reduced the size of the organization and let most of their employees go. Despite the emotional challenges of making such a major change, they found a much better path forward for everyone. Rather than beating themselves up to raise a pile of money each year to sustain a larger-than-necessary organization, they took off all the pressure and just let themselves "be." By seriously addressing the why question, and then acting on the answer, they came to understand their group's true calling and identity. As a result, life almost immediately improved for them all.

We Won't Know If We Don't Ask

We ask "why" because we have something important to learn, and we've realized we won't come to know it unless we ask why. We ask "why," not "what," because "what" will tell us only facts without giving us the context of those facts, or where they fit, or how they interact with other facts, or what difference it all makes. The why gets to every one of those concerns.

When we ask why, we approach a challenging issue with an open mind, determined to genuinely understand the reasons behind our direction, processes or actions. Only by being willing to accept the results of going deep can we ascertain if we do, in fact, fully understand why we've been doing what we've been doing. Only then can we grasp how our current situation affects our ability to move forward.

The process is not about controlling circumstances or allowing circumstances to control us, but rather, learning how to relax into our true position, whatever it really is. It's about accurately gauging where we are, not trying to dictate the outcome of what we discover or predetermining our conclusions based on what we want to believe.

Which reminds me of an old joke.

A man became convinced he was dead. No matter what anyone said to try to convince him otherwise, he insisted, "No, I'm dead." One day his wife took him to the hospital to see if doctors there could prove to him that he really was alive. One very clever physician began by saying, "It's a medical fact that dead people don't bleed." He then showed the man a medical textbook to confirm the claim. Next he took the man to the morgue, where he pricked the limbs of several corpses. None of them bled. "Do you believe that dead people don't bleed?" he asked the man.

"Yes," the man said, "dead people don't bleed."

The doctor then grabbed the man's hand and pricked one of his fingers, which immediately began to bleed. "What does that tell you?" the doctor asked triumphantly.

"Well, my goodness," the man replied. "I guess dead people really do bleed."

When we stop trying to control our circumstances or interpreting data in only one "approved" way, insisting that we see only what we want to see, we significantly enhance our ability to ask and answer the deep questions that help us to focus on how to get better. Rather than being bound by our preconceptions, we discover the freedom to dig deep and to follow the path of the truth, irrespective of where it goes.

The why question, then, is not just more of the same. It is meant to provoke fresh, clear and new thinking. If we settle for expected responses and clichéd answers—the ones that merely repeat the same tired phrases of former times—we almost certainly will not achieve our greatest potential.

I know it's a hard thing to overcome corporate inertia, to change direction when we've been doing something in a certain way for a long time. But unless we dig deep with the why question, maybe bringing in some outside advisors with new perspectives to help us see things in a new way, we tend to become a mere projection of our past. We all need people in our orbit who just might try to nudge us off our current course.

One problem here is that many companies talk incessantly about the importance of "tribal knowledge." They often use that phrase to explain why they avoid bringing in creative new talent, or refuse to hire individuals outside of their industry, or ignore even the possibility that opinions that originated outside of their organization might have something to offer. In my experience, that's how companies go bankrupt, both fiscally and creatively.

One of the most brilliant men I've ever met runs a semi-successful company that should perform far better than it has to date. When he and I first discussed his need to address the why question, he balked. While I believe he knew he had to grapple with the issues, he just couldn't bring himself to do so.

As time marched on and his company began to crumble, he called to ask for another consult. We met, but still he wouldn't seriously address the why question. He's so smart, he can't get past his own intellect. Even to this day, this brilliant man refuses to face into reality. While he believes his company is worth X, it's probably worth only twenty percent of X. I very much hope things work out for him, but until he becomes willing to ask and answer the why question, I doubt any amount of intellect will save his company from imploding.

Why Are You Doing That?

I probably started asking the why question as a very young man. I loved to read and I equally loved to understand what I read. But that love sometimes became a problem for me, because I grew up in a very fundamentalist, legalistic family. Even as a young man, I didn't feel I received good explanations for certain questions.

As a small child, for example, we lived across the street from a Baptist church, but every Sunday morning we drove ten miles to attend a different Baptist church. In those days, schools had "release time" every Wednesday, when you could take an hour off of school to attend religious training classes off campus. So every Wednesday, I went to the Baptist church across the street. Why was it okay to go to that church on Wednesday, I asked my parents, but not on Sunday? I never got a good answer.

From there, my own sense of trying to know why just continued to grow. I kept trying to figure it out. I would listen. Or I would read. Or I would observe. I wanted to know *why*.

When I went to college and then began a career, it became apparent that not many people were asking that question, at least, not like I was. They would do whatever someone told them to do, or they would just accept whatever they were told, like sheep. But so many times I observed those people missing wonderful opportunities to see an issue from a larger context and so bring far more personal meaning to it.

When I first started leading organizations, whether in the business or in the ministry worlds, it quickly became apparent that most people didn't know why they were doing what they were hired to do. Somebody had given them a job description or assigned them some task, and they just did it. They had no idea why that job was important within the context of the larger organization. And so, in more than a few cases, they continued to do the job even when it had ceased to support the organization's goals.

In this regard, I think about Jim. I'd known him only a short while when I hired him to speak at a company event. Not long afterward, Jim asked if I might join him on an Alaska fishing trip. "Can I bring my son?" I asked. He cheerfully agreed.

Weeks before we left, I learned that a group of fifteen to twenty of us would make the trip, a prospect I loved. Not long after we arrived, Jim said to me, "Let's go for a walk." He and I and a third man walked down a long path to a beautiful waterfall. On the way back, Jim started describing some struggles he was having with leadership, including a tough one with a key employee. Although he described Bill as a good man, he told me his skill set and personality no longer seemed to fit the job that Jim needed done.

I responded as I usually do; I began asking the why question. "Why are you letting this persist?" I asked. "Are you doing this because you feel badly for Bill? Or do you feel badly for your organization that some conflict often surrounds him?"

Jim listened, asked questions of his own, and started thinking aloud about his problem. A few days after our group returned home, Jim was able to approach Bill and say, "You know, this just isn't working. It's nothing about you as a person. It's about how you fit within this organization and what we need." Jim didn't look forward to the conversation, but he had it.

Until that time, Jim's frustration had remained at full strength for a long period. Because Jim couldn't answer the why question, he honestly didn't know what to do. But once he understood the why, he found the resolve to quickly take the action required and thus allow his organization to move forward in a healthier direction.

As I've seen happen often, Bill soon landed in a spot much better suited to his skills and personality. So long as Bill remained in Jim's organization, everyone felt frustrated. But once he found a place where he truly fit, everybody breathed a deep sigh of relief.

Asking why can help to reduce or eliminate this type of problem. Asking why, and then acting appropriately on the answer, not only enables the organization to better accomplish its purpose, but almost always makes the workplace more rewarding and fills our people with a deeper sense of joy.

Are You Willing to Get Uncomfortable?

Many of us have a natural aversion to asking why because we suspect, quite rightly, that digging deep to understand the why can bring us to some very uncomfortable places. This is no superficial exercise! It implies change, and many of us dislike all varieties of change.

In my work with many kinds of organizations, I often find that fear is the primary element that fuels a lack of willingness to go to the deep places uncovered by asking why. We fear the changes that our exploration of the why may ask us to make.

I once spoke with the head of a relatively small organization in San Francisco who wanted my help in "fixing" her company.

When I urged her to begin by asking the why question, she made it clear she didn't see any need to go there.

"I just need somebody to tell me what I should do," she said. "I need somebody to write up a business plan or give me some action steps. Then I'll know what to do."

I've followed the progress of her organization from a distance, and so far as I can tell, nothing has changed. If anything, the business has declined. No surprise there. This exec had no ability to be self-reflective, which is part of what the why question demands. How can I dig deep inside of myself to be honest with myself?

My good friends, Drs. Henry Cloud and John Townsend, talk about this issue in terms of "facing our own realities." That's part of what I'm trying to get to when I ask the why question. I want to work at being honest with myself.

While I well understand the fear about facing our own realities, we need to remember that we don't dig deep in order to find negative things. Asking why isn't about encouraging negativity. We ask why because *we seek to understand and fully know what's driving us.* Once we understand the why, we can then begin to understand the next steps toward becoming a better person, a better leader, a better corporation, or a better organization. So yes, asking why can make us feel uncomfortable. I can testify to that! But it also can lead us to a far better place. And isn't that the point?

We All Need to Be Challenged

During my years of serving on the Board of Trustees at Wheaton College, I occasionally challenged some statement or perspective articulated by the president, a very intelligent man. But I always did so with gentleness and respect. He struggled a bit with it at first. But after a time, on more than one occasion, he told me, "Greg, you challenge me in a way that I don't feel personally threatened."

That's really important when dealing anyone, but especially with high profile people. Most of them think, *I'm really smart and I already know the answer, so don't tell me something I don't want to hear.* They often closely attach their egos to what they do and where they sit. And even when they say, "It's not about me," everyone in the room can see (except they themselves) that it really is about them.

As leaders, we need others to challenge us. It's vital if we are to get at the truth. Honest dialogue lies at the core of asking the why question. We must encourage the truth to be spoken, although we also need to remind ourselves and others that it's easier to receive when it's delivered gently and respectfully. And when we find ourselves on the receiving end of uncomfortable truth, we also need to learn how to accept it with grace, for if we can't receive the truth gratefully, then all our credibility vanishes.

A man named Lane once reported to me. He headed up our marketing/advertising division. Early on, I said to him, "Lane, I need you to challenge me. You may think that if I say, 'This is the answer,' then that is the answer and I don't want any more discussion. But I need you to challenge me, to make sure that we're doing the right things. I can't promise you that I'll always do what you recommend, but I'll listen. And if I don't, you also need to tell me that."

I knew that if somebody appropriately challenged me and I replied, "What in the world are you talking about? That's a crazy idea," no one would ever challenge me again. So I not only had to work to remain self-aware on the issue, but I also needed to solicit others to keep me accountable to my commitment to get at the truth of the why. As a result, our company became a lot better. I never could have done it by myself.

She Needs to Know Why

Throughout my career, I've wanted those with whom I had the closest working relationships to know what I was doing and why

I was doing it. Such an approach didn't always sit well with some of my colleagues. I used to buck heads with a few individuals who said, "Greg, you're sharing too much. You know, we need to be confidential about this. Your assistants don't need to know that."

I would typically respond, "Sometimes, those are the very people who have the ability to help us do a better job—but how can they help us if they don't know the bigger picture? Why torpedo what we want to accomplish by failing to give our people the information that could help us to succeed?"

I also insisted, "I'm going to lead by example. I'm going to share more rather than less. I'll take that risk. Because if I do, I think we'll get better results." Did I ever get burned? Sure, I did. But I have very little doubt that my approach worked better than the alternative, even when running a large organization.

Shortly after I hired a favorite long-time assistant, Heather, I told her, "I'm not going to try to decide what you can know and what you can't know. Therefore, you're going to know everything about everything that comes in and out of this office. There's not one thing I won't trust with you. You get one time that you inappropriately use something you've learned here and share it somewhere else, and then you'll be done. So those are the rules up front, just so you know."

Heather did an outstanding job. When she walked into my office, I didn't have to worry about hiding or covering up something sensitive lying on my desk. She knew enough about what was going on that she could also forewarn me about critical issues coming my way.

When we trust those closest to us, when we help them to become part of the why, their jobs become more significant to them, and as a result, they often become a major force in helping the organization to succeed. Their own lives get to be different, and better.

To this day, I know that former colleagues and co-workers all over the country are still asking the why question in their corporations and businesses. Some have moved from one company to another, always bringing with them that desire to know why—not to cause problems in the new organization or to make people feel uncomfortable, but to enable that organization, business or church to get better.

A Religious Reluctance to Ask Why

In my view, the non-profit Christian world, by and large, doesn't do a very good job of asking the why question. In working with both churches and ministries, I've observed a great fear of facing into their own reality, a deep reluctance to be really honest with themselves about their organizations. In most cases, it's because they know that if they grasped the real truth—if they honestly came to grips with their own reality—then they would have to do something different. They would have to change. And the idea of change scares them. So they pretend, cloaking their refusal to deal with their reality in a blizzard of spiritual-sounding verbiage.

Until reality gives them no options.

Most of the time, these organizations see few major consequences of refusing to ask the why question . . . at least immediately. For a while, it can seem like everything is going well, and in many ways, it is. But they don't grasp that as well as things seem to be going, they could be going much better—a very important difference. Almost never do they say, "We want to be the very best we can be," whatever that "best" is. And so they accept mediocrity and call it God's will.

Before too long, however, they hit a plateau. And eventually, something unpleasant happens that forces a major shift in leadership. It is, of course, almost never a very good leadership transition, because a forced action usually results in a mess.

The fact is, asking the why question is not a threat, but frees us to become even more of what we really want to be. Far from sending us over the cliff, asking the why question enables us to reach our heart's desire. Too many significant leaders in ministry fear to go deep. They assume that what they will discover there is likely to be negative, rather than something that frees them to become even more.

One of the best answers I've found for dealing with this kind of fear lies with the board of an organization. I like working with boards, because in my view, boards are the weakest link for the church, not the pastor. The pastor reflects only what the board allows him or her to be. A good board can make a huge difference in the life of a church or ministry organization.

So why is it, then, that while we discuss endlessly how to help the pastor grow, or the staff grow, or our programs grow, we rarely think much about helping board members to grow?

We usually say our board members should be the spiritual leaders of the church, rather than saying we need individuals who can make up a well-rounded board, members who also have a strong spiritual commitment. I believe a church board should strive to have the right kind of gift mix to cover the entirety of what the organization is about. Does the board have people who reflect all the various parts of the church? In my experience, that often doesn't happen.

Who on the board has strong financial skills? Who has good ability in communication? Who has a gift of giving (quite a few non-profit boards focus on that one)? Who has only a few resources? I've long thought that a board needs at least one member who reflects the kind of people the church serves, which in many cases means someone who has little money. Some of the best board members I've known are people who had to be subsidized. They tend to have a unique perspective that needs a careful hearing.

I really struggle with boards designed the way some megachurch pastors think they should be designed. A few years ago, I was asked to observe a meeting where one such pastor described to a group of twenty-five other megachurch pastors how they should deal with board members who want to present ideas for consideration that lay outside of the pastor's vision. It absolutely blew me away.

The pastor stood over a colleague sitting in a corner and said, "You have thirty seconds to shut that down so that you don't lose control of your board. You don't want to let them have any kind of conversation that might lead in a direction different from where you want to go." He did his little spiel and then sat down.

I don't entirely blame the pastor for his power play, since I don't see it as a pastoral thing, but as a human thing. Almost all of us have a tendency to protect ourselves. We try very hard to prevent someone from shooting down an idea of ours, because it feels like shooting us down. And the more authority we have, the more we struggle in this arena. We may think, *if even subconsciously, If you say something negative about my idea or suggest a different option, then you're destroying my dream.*

In religious organizations, of course, many leaders often say, "God's given me a vision." In doing so, they ignore the fact that if it's only *their* vision and not affirmed by a whole bunch of others, we should have some deep suspicions about it. The why question, if taken seriously, can go a long way toward righting such a listing ship.

I once sat on a board where I got to know an African American pastor. He'd joined the board a few years before I did. During breaks and lunches, I started sitting next to him and we started to become friends. I wanted to know more about him and what he did.

It turned out he was about to become the presiding bishop of his denomination, a very conservative, Black evangelical church. One day he said to me, "Greg, for all the years I've been on this board, no one's ever just talked to me as a person. I know I'm here because I'm black and because I fill out a particular demographic." That was hard for me to hear. While I believe it's important to have people of color as part of any organization, to ignore them reflects a serious leadership issue.

My friend eventually started asking me to help him figure out some denominational problems, all because I showed an interest in him and asked a few questions, especially the why question. I've been to his church any number of times and we still periodically have lunch together. His board can sometimes make life hard for him—he once moved the communion table one foot, for example, and the board blew him up for it—and I can help act as a "safe" sounding board for him.

No one on his board lives in the neighborhood where the church's facilities are located. Some of them drive up to fifty miles to attend that church, but they don't want to live anywhere near it. While the neighborhood has declined, the church building sits on a beautiful piece of property. My friend finds himself in a difficult position. And unfortunately, other than encouraging him to try to get some new members on his board, I don't have many answers for him.

I might have one answer, but it would be very difficult for him to implement in that church. What the church desperately needs is a long, hard, serious exploration of the why question. Why do they do what they do? Why do no board members live within fifty miles of the church? Why is moving the communion table one foot such a big deal? Uncomfortable questions, sure. But until they get asked and answered, that church can't hope for more than mediocrity. Reaching for better almost always requires us to go deep on the why.

New Lessons to Learn

Men and women who want to be all-in leaders need to recognize that they always have some new lesson to learn. There's always something they haven't thought about. Asking the why question is about learning, and especially about becoming honestly self-reflective. It's about digging deep to discover an important truth that may lie hidden or obscured, so that we can deal effectively with reality and move toward a better place for us within it.

One of the leaders I coach wrote an interesting blog in response to a question I'd posed to him, a question that apparently caused him no small amount of distress. "Why are you doing this?" I had asked. "Are you doing it because it's best for your business, or because you want to be right?" He had often admitted publicly that he likes being right and hates being wrong, so he found my question very uncomfortable to process. He wrote,

> My thoughts ran forward to how much damage I might do to my lifetime impact potential. What if I don't have the maturity to do the wise thing, even when it means being wrong in my eyes or someone else's? The foolish choices I could make in the name of being right scare me.
>
> Leaders need to be resilient. Part of that is having the security to admit a wrong, or tolerate being called wrong, and not let that interfere with wise decision-making.

I asked this leader the why question because I wanted him to get to the essence of a critical topic that I knew could make or break his business. I wanted him to think more clearly about how, moving forward, he would act and conduct his business and relationships.

I had no preconditions when I asked the question. I did not attempt to influence his answer. I asked "why" only to prompt him to think more deeply and with greater clarity, so he could better accomplish what he said he wanted to accomplish.

"I'm really thankful he asked me that tough question," this exec wrote. Despite the discomfort it caused him, he, explained that it brought up "one of the most important lessons I can learn at this point in my leadership career."

Good leaders never stop learning. They continually ask why, even when they know it will make them uncomfortable, because they want to grapple with reality and not simply play with fiction. They value new lessons, because they know those lessons will equip them and their organizations to succeed and get better.

Asking and answering the why question doesn't end the learning, however. In large measure, it simply sets the table for the next course of learning. Once you know why you're doing something, the next question is, "How can I do it better?"

How Can We Do Better?

I can't say I'm a techie. I like gadgets and I have a few of them, but I'm not the type who will camp out overnight at the local Apple store, waiting for the newest whiz-bang device to arrive.

Nevertheless, I really like what Robert Brunner said back in 2014 at the Gigaom Roadmap conference. Brunner, the founder of the Ammunition design studio—which works with lightweight clients such as Adobe, Ferrari, Intel, Microsoft and others, and which in February 2015 *Fast Company* named as the world's most innovative design company—told his audience that the world has entered a "time of confusion and ill-conceived stuff." He had in mind the avalanche of digital devices and gadgets that attempt to connect people in various ways. Brunner gave five bits of counsel on how to create well-conceived stuff rather than ill-conceived stuff, and at least one of those pieces of advice strongly resonated with me.

Brunner told the crowd, "Make it a better thing: Different is not enough. A connected device should truly make its users' lives better."

Better, not just different—that's also the mantra of the second big question. Once you've asked why you're doing what you're doing and work through it to find a satisfying answer, then it's time to move to the next step. You ask yourself, "How can we do better?"

Not Change for Change's Sake

If we spend the time and energy to address *why* we are engaged in some function or task, then wouldn't it be silly not to address *how* we might be able to do it better? We are not interested in change for change's sake. We want to know how we can improve, advance, progress toward the goals we have set for ourselves.

I believe it's vital to make this distinction between "better" and "different," because most of us tend naturally to think in terms of "different" rather than "better." We live in an age in which we hear continually how one value or approach or method is not necessarily better than any other, but merely different. That sentiment is part of the air we breathe. You know: "I like vanilla, you like strawberry; neither your choice nor mine is better, just different." And that's a totally legitimate perspective in a large number of contexts.

We run into problems, however, when we transport that mindset wholesale into the operation of our businesses. If something we're doing hasn't worked quite right, then we need to discover what might work better, not merely what we could do differently. If we simply do something differently, without asking ourselves whether it will help us to do better, we might easily wind up in a far worse condition than before we started. "Differently" lacks the focus and power of "better." We want to grow stronger, more effective, healthier . . . *better*.

And once we make changes, "different" simply doesn't help us to see if the changes we've made actually worked to help us get further down the track. Since we're on a journey to seek the best possible outcomes for our organizations, we want to know what (and how) we can do better, not merely what we might do in another way. We ask "how can we do better" not to seek perfection, but to understand in what ways we might improve what we do and how we can enhance our operations.

Asking this question played a big role in how I advised a man who had spent many years in the military. He thought the time might have come for him to find a suitable position in the business world. Right from the start, I told him, "I think you may have to change some of the ways you tend to interact with others, which will take a conscious adjustment on your part. Maybe it would help to talk through these issues if you and I and our wives could have dinner together. I'd also like to hear some things about what your spouse may be interested in you doing professionally after your military career."

"Okay," he said, "why don't you come to our house for dinner?"

"Great," I replied. He told me that he'd send an email with directions to his home; and when it arrived, I noticed that the note came from a captain. A little detail, maybe, but it seemed to have a direct connection to the "better" question. So I called him back.

"I just want you to know," I said, "that if you go into the civilian world, you will not have a captain-level person writing emails for you to give directions to a visitor. It doesn't work that way. A captain is a high, midlevel management person, right?"

"I suppose that's right," he answered.

"Well, it's not going to be that way. You'll have some administrative person doing tasks like this. You're used to an environment that allows you to utilize individuals who have reached very high levels to do work that often doesn't reflect on their core capacity. You're going to have to think through how you might have to do tasks like this, not merely in a different way, but in a better way more suited to the new environment, whatever that environment ends up being."

Better, not just different. That's the question.

Focus on the Essential, not Merely the Preferential

Part of the better question forces us to consider carefully the core of what we do, not merely the most enjoyable or easiest or most satisfying parts of what we do. Too often we mistakenly focus on the preferential issues and not primarily on the essential issues, which tends to fix our attention on the nearest term problem to be resolved.

But what if the nearest term issue clamoring for our attention lacks anything like the importance of a core issue, which may require greater investigation but has a far greater ability to influence our organizational health? Finding solutions to the core, long-term issues we face ultimately make the biggest difference to our corporate health.

I once helped a business called kitchenCRATE to think through some of these issues. The company specializes in affordable, durable, eye-catching kitchen remodels at rates often less than half the norm. It had done very well in its region and the owners wanted to start franchising—but the company hadn't yet really solidified its core business. It needed to back away from those plans a bit until it had formed a much clearer idea of what it did best. Once it focused on its core and knew exactly what it had to offer, it had the ability to develop a great business plan that paved the way for its current success.

Not Always a Straight Line

While asking the "how can we do better" question tends to lead us in a certain direction, only rarely do we reach our intended destination via a straight line. Life just isn't like that. It's more often made up of little, subtle meanderings. Asking and answering the how question, therefore, normally results in a continual series of small course corrections, not a major leap.

Almost certainly, some of the new things we try will work, while some others won't. Or maybe those attempts won't work today, but perhaps they might in the future. And so we engage in a constant banging around, assessing not only our situation in the moment, but also trying to understand what's coming down the road and how far we've come.

Asking the "how" question doesn't necessarily imply we'll need to make substantive, even massive, changes. Usually, it's more helpful to think in terms of nuanced change. While some companies may indeed require major and immediate change, leadership on a day-to-day basis is far more about being able to articulate and execute small, nuanced changes. We live in a world of nuance, and normally the majority of the changes we need to make belong to that category. The idea is that through nuanced change, we're trying to become better, a little bit at a time.

A few years ago, United Airlines was looking for a new president. One day, someone on the search committee called to talk to me about the process. "What if we don't find anybody who has everything we're looking for?" he asked.

"Well," I said, "I think you can find that person. But even if you don't, that doesn't mean that other people in the organization can't, in the interim, do at least pieces of what's required. If you don't find everything you're looking for at once, you can still move ahead with some changes until you find what you really need."

In other words, you don't have to wait to act until you have everything in place. Little changes that start moving you in the right direction can start almost anywhere. And these smaller changes tend to have a morphing effect that travel everywhere, paving the way for the bigger changes to come so that they seem more feasible and less frightening.

Nuanced changes, of course, by themselves don't normally accomplish the large-scale goals we may have set for ourselves. When they don't, it's natural to start saying to ourselves, "Man, we haven't gotten there! We've been trying new things, but we haven't reached the place we really want." As we look back at where we've been, however, we begin to see that we've actually made quite a lot of progress. We're not where we once were; we've moved to a better place.

Don't let it bother you, therefore, if you can't immediately find an exhaustive answer about how to do something better. Make it your goal to find and execute at least some piece of that "better." As you find and execute more of those pieces, you can fill in the blanks along the way. Refuse to waste too much of your energy addressing something that you can't quite put your hands around.

Think of someone trying to move from Point A to Point F. When the individual gets to Point E, he may think he's not moved very far, since he's not yet where he wants to be. But when he stops to reflect, he sees he's really moved from A to B, then to C, then to D, and then to E—not all the way just yet, but still, quite a long ways. Since he's been at it for a while, he may feel as if he's just wandering . . . but he's not. He's moving ahead, moving toward the goal. Becoming aware of that movement can give the individual the momentum and encouragement he needs to keep going toward the desired goal, even if it happens in a series of small steps.

Not long ago, I spoke to a leader about this very issue. He was bemoaning some things, lamenting that he hadn't accomplished all he'd set out to do. Rather than reflect on his process, he tended to obsess over it. And so I told him, "It's great to reflect, but look how far you've come. You need to turn your attention quickly back toward where you need to go." Small steps, with your eyes locked on the goal.

Challenge and Support

This ongoing process of asking and answering the how question is about both challenge and support—challenging the status quo, while supporting those we lead. Either one without the other can freeze your progress.

I wrestled a bit in college. At some tournaments, you might wrestle two or three times in a day. Every opponent, of course, had different habits, styles, strengths and weaknesses. So after I finished one match, I had to get ready for the next one. Whether I won or lost, I needed to evaluate how I had performed in the previous match and then get ready for the contest coming up. I couldn't afford to obsess on what I had done, whether well or poorly, because I had to prepare for the new challenge ahead of me. But I did have to analyze what had just happened and then mentally look forward to get ready for the upcoming match. In effect, I had to both challenge myself and support myself.

A similar dynamic is true in business. I want to act as a "healthy skeptic." Healthy, in that I'm finding ways to support my people as they pursue our goal. Skeptical, in that I don't necessarily believe we've found the best answer after just one or two attempts to articulate an appropriate response. I want us to keep digging even as I provide healthy support for the team and the process.

The danger at this stage is that some may perceive our skepticism as sarcasm or as unhelpful criticism. We have to watch very carefully what we're conveying not only through our words, but also through our body language and verbal tone. If we say "nice doggie" but bare our teeth and pick up a whip, we are unlikely to elicit the outcome we desire. For this reason, our integrity becomes critical here, requiring us to make certain that our questioning comes out of a genuine desire to find and implement the "better." We've drifted off point if we ask the questions simply to engage in some one-upmanship. Our questions may, in fact, sting a little at times; but they never do so simply to make us look superior.

A man I knew died unexpectedly of a heart attack several weeks ago. His boss never called the grieving widow, so I called him this week to say, "this man's widow needs some closure. Didn't he work for you for twenty-seven years in middle management?"

"Yeah," he replied, "he worked for me and he was my friend."

"How can you say he's your friend," I asked, "when you don't even call the widow?"

"Well, we didn't think she really wanted all of that," he answered, a little sheepishly. He seemed totally clueless how important it would be to bring closure for this man's widow. And then he told me, "We created this book of remembrance and people signed it and talked about the great things he did"—but somehow, the widow never received the book. Now, it was a really good thing that they created this book, but how much better if the widow actually got to see it?

Sometimes, our challenge and support has to sting a bit if the "better" is ever to see the light of day.

Through such a process of questioning, we all begin to gain a sharper understanding of the problem that we can share with others for our mutual benefit. Asking the questions gives us a golden opportunity to prove that we're truly intent on discovering how we can help to make things better. I like to think of it as trying to uncover the rest of the story.

My son-in-law, a recent university graduate, has entered the business world and has significant aspirations for his career. During our regular times together, I repeatedly ask the "how" question. I do this to help him understand the key issues. I want him to grasp the questions he needs to ponder so he can wrestle through to his own conclusions about his professional growth. He tells me that our sessions are helping him to understand the thought processes he needs if he is to build the kind of career and life he truly wants.

Like most young executives, he has a strong desire to get noticed by his superiors. So sometimes we discuss ideas regarding how to get noticed, as well as some cautionary thoughts on what *not* to do. I never tell him what he should do, but rather focus on helping him know the right questions and recognizing the proper sequence of questions. I try to help him to see some of his options in accomplishing his short-term goals, as well as assisting him in clarifying his ultimate long-term goal and how he might move toward it. Since I'm not him or in his circumstances, I avoid telling him what I'd do. I'm there to ask the questions and to walk alongside him as he reflects on his options, again, giving both challenge and support. I help him to determine for himself what course of action might best enable him to move ahead in his organization and career.

Collaborative by Nature

Asking the how question is collaborative by nature. I know some doubt that leaders can lead effectively by being collaborative, but my experience has taught me that through the process of asking the how question in a collaborative way, we can usually reach a decision that strongly resonates with both the leader and those being led.

When your colleagues rightly believe that they have been part of the decision-making process, they tend to more quickly and strongly align themselves with the decisions so made. Most people, myself included, want to be heard. We all want to be part of the process of deciding where our organization is going and how it gets there.

So what do you do when you realize your organization or company needs to make some changes? What if you've drifted from your mission or your vision (your current strategy to help you accomplish your mission) needs an overhaul? How do you move from one place to another—always seeking the better—without causing widespread panic or even risking collapse?

A friend of mine, Peter Greer, serves as president and CEO of Hope International, a Christian ministry that fosters microenterprise in underdeveloped regions of the world. He and his director of development, Chris Horst, wrote a helpful book titled *Mission Drift* that both *Christianity Today* and *World* magazine named 2015 leadership book of the year. They demonstrate how easy it is for groups to drift away from their core mission and so lose their way. And if you lose sight of your core mission, your vision for fulfilling your mission becomes confused at best and unworkable at worst.

Suppose, though, that you have not drifted from your mission, but your old vision no longer gets you where you want to be, whether because times have changed, the culture has shifted, or something else. You have to turn around your organization by shifting your strategy. What can you do?

The world of communication studies has given us an extremely helpful tool that many corporations and businesses have used over the past few decades to help them make exactly this kind of turnaround. Symbolic Convergence Theory (SCT) suggests that leaders who want to create a new vision for their companies, or reinvigorate a fading one, must find a way to synthesize their ideas and desires with those of the rank and file. It rarely works simply to impose a new vision from above. Instead, the viewpoints of the leader's associates must bubble up from below at the same time that the leader's viewpoints trickle down from above. One of the best ways to encourage this kind of bubbling effect is by asking the how question, over and over.

Effective leaders use this new mix to create a purposeful new construct that incorporates elements from both "above" and "below." And then they begin the process of finding compelling new terms to express this fresh vision, tasking gifted speakers to articulate it, tapping appropriate channels to convey it, creating special events to celebrate it, and so forth. In other words, these leaders invite collaboration even as they help to direct its course. In that way, everyone together discovers a better way forward for the entire organization.

Does it work? Indeed it does. Many journal articles describe how SCT has helped businesses turn around their fortunes[1], and a large number of resources outline how struggling organizations have used even pieces of the approach to dramatic effect. For example, a slumping Reuters recorded losses of almost 500 million

---

1   For example, see Cragan, John F., & Shields, Donald C. (1992). The Use of Symbolic Convergence Theory in Corporate Strategic Planning: A Case Study. *Journal of Applied Communication Research.* (20)2, 199-218.

pounds in 2002, prompting its CEO to describe the company as "fighting for survival." Only one year later, it recorded *profits* of almost 500 million pounds. "Communication was at the heart of this remarkable recovery," wrote a company executive. Reuters designed and executed a special one-day event that included all its offices in more than 140 countries. The event involved live video feeds, Q&A sessions, a special website, toolkits, teasers prior to the event, and locally organized social activities after the event. "Feedback from employees both on and following the day was overwhelmingly positive. Even the CEO described it as 'the day the company turned the corner,'" said an executive.[2]

When we spend time asking significant questions of our colleagues, they quickly come to know that we believe in them. Among other things, the exercise tends to improve the quality of their responses. When we consistently ask discerning, thoughtful questions, we demonstrate our belief in our people and show our loyalty to them, which leads to stronger, more effective organizations.

Too many leaders think they need to provide answers rather than ask questions. A few years ago, Philip K. Howard wrote a book titled *The Death of Common Sense*. "For too long," he declared, "we have been training leaders who know only how to keep the routine going. Who can answer questions but don't know how to ask them."

Most leaders want to be people of influence. But to be effective as a leader, your ability to ask the right question at the right time is critical. By asking questions, especially the how question, you help to clarify your own thinking, which enables you to better lead. The right questions also bring out our colleagues' best thinking. The intent is to find the best answers together, along with the best solutions and the best opportunities involving the least amount of risk.

---

2   Bell, Anne Marie. (2005). Inspiring organizational change at Reuters. *Strategic Communication Management*. Aug/Sep (9)5; 18-22.

Comfortable May Not Mean Better

One of the worst assumptions we can make about our lives and businesses sounds like this: "What we've always done, we should always do." While the familiar approach may feel more comfortable for a while, its warm comfort disappears the moment it stops working.

And so we ask the central question, "how can we do this better," even when it means challenging the conventional or reexamining the status quo. Could such a challenge result in a time of heightened discomfort? No question.

A friend recently described a long interchange with the senior pastor of the church he attended at the time. The pastor was feverishly trying to figure out why his church was declining, a drop of more than 1,500 regular attenders in less than ten years. This leader's answers always pointed to other staff people: "It must be the worship guy's fault," "It must be the youth guy's fault." Several times he insisted, "It can't be me. I'm doing everything just as I've always done it."

My friend told me, "There were two problems with that. First, it was a new day, and many of the old approaches had stopped working. And second, I didn't think it was true. I didn't believe he still was doing some of the things he used to do so effectively." The pastor's central problem? He refused to take an unflinching, honest look at what might truly help his church to reach a better place. He rejected any hint that he might lie at the heart of some of the church's biggest problems. Seasons came and went, the church continued to decline, and eventually the pastor lost his job.

I've met with any number of business leaders who have spoken to me almost the same words as this pastor. "We had great success doing *this*," they insisted. "I'm still doing the same thing, so if we're not successful today, *I* can't be the reason. It must be someone else's fault."

You can find all kinds of examples of such willful blindness in the business world. Think of the automotive industry, or the world of high tech, or the computer industries. Think of Word Perfect, Lotus, AOL. They once ruled their niches, but they didn't continue to make the changes they needed to. They lost their head starts and now they're gone.

They all had good products, but they didn't adapt soon enough and competing firms moved more quickly. Many of these endangered companies continued to say, right up until they imploded, "But this is really working. People love us. So we're good."

This sort of repeated, intentional blindness just described suggests why we must continually ask ourselves, "how can we do better?" We must be willing to dig deep, even if it leads to frightening places that might feel uncomfortable, even painful. Continually asking, "How can we do this better?" can shine a bright light exactly where some growing shadows have been obscuring our vision.

Don't Be a Sheep

When I worked in the commercial real estate investment market, I discovered a truism that tripped up a lot of good leaders. It went like this:

If we all do the same thing,
I can't be held accountable if we all go in the wrong direction.

Leaders can't afford to thoughtlessly go with the flow or to mindlessly follow the crowd. They can't be sheep. They must train themselves to think more clearly, more deeply, and more independently, so they can help their people and their organizations achieve the larger objective. And we get to that clearer, deeper, and more independent thought primarily by asking the question "how."

We leaders can't afford to act like sheep. In fact, we will find it very hard to reach our "better" if we simply go wherever the sheep in front of us go, or where our own inclinations want us to go.

Thomas Edison has an earned reputation in American history for his creativity and doggedness in invention. A favorite story tells how he visited a bank one day to get funding for a new creation, the phonograph. The banker threw him out of his office, yelling, "get that toy out of here!" Edison persisted, of course, and his invention led eventually to things like Walkmans and iPods and cell phones that play music not only in your parlour, but in your earbuds as you walk down the street.

Many of us know that story, but not as many of us, perhaps, know that Edison never made his phonograph into a profitable business. The Victor Talking Machine Company and several other competitors took the lion's share of the market; in 1919, Edison's company produced only 7.2 percent of the phonographs made in the U.S. and 11.3 percent of the records, and by the end of the 1920s, his market share of the record business had dipped to a measly 2 percent. Why?

In a nutshell, Edison didn't ask the how question broadly enough. He focused on making his machines technically superior, but scorned any idea of asking the public what it really wanted. While Victor widely used popular singers of the day to promote its product, for example, Edison declared in a 1912 memorandum, "We care nothing for the reputation of the artists, singers or instrumentalists. All that we desire is that the voice shall be as perfect as possible."

He got what he wanted. Sort of. Historians generally agree that he did produce the best-sounding, most technically-proficient phonographs on the market. So bully for him. But Edison's record-making company went out of business in 1929.

(Can you say, "Betamax"?)

How and Mission & Vision

Questions have a way of almost automatically engaging people on a practical level. Have you ever wondered why effective leaders tend to ask so many questions? It's not necessarily that they're looking for information. Often, it's because their questions get people to engage with some reality that either they've ignored or misunderstood. To get them re-engaged, these leaders don't give them lectures; they ask them questions.

In exactly the same way, the right questions can help to effectively engage your people in the mission and vision of your organization. The first big question, "Why am I doing this," corresponds in many ways to mission. It gets to the very core of why you're doing something in the first place. So by asking the question, the abstract concept ("mission") becomes more practical ("why are you doing this?").

The second big question, "How can we do this better," corresponds in many ways to vision. While mission tends to change very little over time, vision changes much more rapidly, according to shifts in environment, economics, style, etc. And so by asking the question, the abstract concept ("vision") becomes more practical ("how can we do this better?").

Only a few core elements are essentially immutable; that's the mission piece. But the vision piece—how we can best accomplish that mission in a changing environment—has to change over time. Elements of the original vision may remain, but we have to reconsider it much more regularly, to ensure that it still reflects current realities and challenges. Continually asking, "how can we do this better" can do nothing but sharpen and strengthen our vision.

While I've served on many boards where we periodically discussed the organization's mission and vision, rarely have I seen these discussions make a practical difference in what the organization actually did. We would talk briefly about mission and vision, and then we'd be off to tackle two or three action steps on some other issue. For the most part, the mission and vision statements of the organization got written up and placed in a three-ring binder, where they stayed.

How many in your organization or on your board can quickly

and accurately articulate your mission and vision? In most organizations, they can't do it. They'll answer, "Well, we put it in the bulletin," or "I know where it is in in our employee handbook." But that's not the point.

It's the leader's responsibility to make sure that people in the organization know the words of the mission and vision and understand what they mean and how the organization intends to put them into practice. And that brings us right back to the two big questions, "why are we doing what we're doing" and "how can we do better?"

Get Yourself Unstuck

A friend of mine has worked for many years in the education world. He recently wrote to me, "I remember the after-hours debriefs that we'd go through, with Bob leading us to evaluate the day using the two big questions. Sometimes, the discussions got hot and personal; but always with our eyes on making the next day and the next delivery better and even more effective. After dinner, by design, we frequently met with attendees at the bar. The time was always aimed at building relationships, supporting them, and positioning the company as a Franchisor or Corporate Owner that always operated in the best interest of all the companies."

My friend's story reminds me that, *Asking and answering the two big questions helps organizations to get unstuck.*

A variety of things can happen when we don't ask the two big questions, and none of them are good. If we want to become the very best we can be, then we have to learn to continuously ask, "why are we doing this?" and "how can we do this better?" The alternative is to accept mediocrity.

Nor do we ask and answer the two big questions and then stop, as if we've mastered a quiz. We ask them, and then ask them again, and then ask them again. The questions provide fodder for a continual cycle of asking and answering. We want to understand the impact of our choices, to gain the ability to weigh one option against another. We want to begin to understand not only the intended consequences of our past decisions, but also the unintended ones, and how we can apply this new knowledge to the decisions currently before us.

Thus, there is no "end of the story" to this process. It's a never-ending cycle. We keep asking the questions because we keep finding new answers in a constantly changing world. And so we keep asking, "Why are we doing this? Where are we today?" and "How can we do this better? Where do we really want to go and how can we best get there?"

Consistently asking the two big questions will markedly enhance your ability as a leader to make a major difference in your organization. Learning to persistently ask and answer these questions gives you a clarity of purpose that allows you to distinguish between merely interesting ideas and those that are truly influential.

Individuals with whom I worked decades ago tell me they're still using the two questions, for one reason: They know they work. We haven't labored together in the same company for a long time, but they keep asking those two questions in firm after firm and organization after organization, because the questions have the simple power to improve the dynamics of their companies.

Why are we doing what we're doing?

How can we do better?

Those two questions create the setting that allows the Five I's to do their own potent work.

Inquisitiveness

*What Seems Irrelevant Today
Becomes Critical Tomorrow*

S ome time ago I read a book titled *In the Garden of the Beast*, by Eric Larson. I had a keen interest in discovering what led up to Nazi Germany's catastrophic choices in World War II. My wife is German and many of her extended family members lived through that horrific period. I didn't read the book merely to learn important facts; much more than that, I desired to really dig in and try to better understand a unique and terrible time in history.

By the time I put down the book, I found that my inquisitiveness had paid off. I came away with a far greater comprehension of a watershed era. Many of those lessons will stay with me for the rest of my life.

I love the process of knowing, of thinking. I'm intrigued by the possibility of acquiring a broad base of knowledge that allows me to interact with a wide assortment of people. I attribute this thirst for knowledge partly to an education based in the liberal arts, but partly to my observation that success more regularly comes to those who enter every situation in an inquisitive manner, with a broad desire to learn and to ask questions. I've learned that what we try to understand may seem irrelevant today, but it has a way of becoming relevant tomorrow.

Inquisitiveness lies at the core of everything. It's really about being genuinely interested in the other. When we take an interest in the other and stop focusing on us alone, we begin to understand that something else "out there" can make our lives more complete and whole.

Inquisitiveness is the process of planting, watering, fertilizing, weeding and harvesting ideas so that the leader's knowledge base blossoms and grows, resulting in a bumper crop of achievement. As leaders, our curiosity must reflect a genuine interest in learning new things. It is not about pretense or a show; rather, good leaders have a fundamental, basic curiosity to learn what we hadn't known. By being curious, we continue to be humbled by what we don't know, but also intrigued by what we have yet to learn.

Observe, Converse, Read

The successful leaders I know all stoke their curiosity through three main channels: Observation, conversation, and reading. All three channels are crucial in the care and feeding of our inquisitiveness.

Observation

Whenever I walk into a room, I try to notice what's there. If it's somebody's office, I want to know, what does it tell me about the person? What kind of pictures does he have? What does she have on her desk? Is it messy? Is it neat? Is it inviting or is it sterile? I can learn a great many things just by observing.

While we can't all be Renaissance people, all of us can be curious. We can all develop a genuine curiosity to really *see* this amazing world.

I was with a friend today who twice wondered aloud about some construction project at a local restaurant. He wanted to walk around the site to see what he could learn. That's inquisitiveness. It had nothing to do with our discussions. He could have remained totally oblivious to the activity, not even noticed it, and it would have made no obvious difference to our interactions. But his curiosity reflects a way he habitually interacts with the world.

In my early business career, I helped manage a small office building near O'Hare airport outside of Chicago. The modern-for-its-time facility featured electric baseboard heating as well as forced air conditioning. One day I observed that each office had two thermostats, one for the air conditioning and one for heating. That surprised me. Later, I noticed that both systems could go on simultaneously. The heating units would try to warm up the room while the air conditioning would try to cool it down.

When I asked our engineers about this, the situation baffled them as much as it did me. But in subsequent months, the manufacturer discovered a way for one thermostat to control both units, resulting in significant cost savings and more comfort for building occupants.

Conversation

Conversations imply learning, unless we remain totally oblivious. Every time we speak with someone, we engage in some aspect of learning. Inquisitiveness is about keeping an open mind in regard to what we hear, about being willing to say, "That's interesting to me. Tell me more."

During my tenure at Coldwell Banker Corporation, we wanted to discover what our employees, agents and franchisees were most interested in learning. We very intentionally began having conversations to learn from these individuals what kind of information they thought might help them perform their jobs more effectively. It soon became apparent that we needed to take a more holistic approach to our education programs.

As a result, the company moved its primary training program, Coldwell Banker University, away from a traditional training and development orientation and toward a more curiosity-based framework. We began to see education, being curious, as analogous to planting seeds. Seeds planted in the soil take time to germinate. Similarly, many times the things we learn must germinate inside our brains. While the germination process occurs, we have to continue to water the seed, fertilize it, keep the weeds out and ultimately reap a harvest. As we learn new ideas through inquisitiveness, those ideas get planted as seeds; and as we continue to be inquisitive, we continue the process of watering, fertilizing, weeding and harvesting, so that eventually our knowledge base grows and we become more effective in everything we do.

Many of the individuals who took part in that CBU initiative so many years ago tell me they're still using and implementing these ideas about curiosity. What was pioneering back then has become the norm several decades later.

Curiosity, inquisitiveness, is the beginning point. Learn to be naturally curious in your conversations and start to hear and learn things you didn't hear and learn before.

Reading

I always find it interesting when people come to my home, because regardless of their background, we find something out of my library to discuss. It could be science. It could be sociology. It could be politics, biography, faith, business books. There's poetry. There's a little bit of everything. All of it comes out of this strong sense of valuing curiosity. Reading widely helps me to think critically and reminds me that what seems irrelevant today often becomes critical tomorrow.

At the suggestion of a mutual friend, a scientist from the Jet Propulsion Laboratory once called me and asked to meet. "Can I send you a draft of my book?" he asked. I agreed. I'm gullible; I read whatever anybody sends me. He'd written a 300 page manuscript dealing with quantum mechanics and faith, a subject very far outside of my experience.

I slowly worked my way through the text and ended up telling him, "I know you worked really hard on this. But you wrote three books, not one. You wrote one book to scientists; it's so technical that nobody else will understand it. You wrote another book on Christian discipleship. And you have a third one for 'seekers.' All of it is intermingled. You really need to work on whichever one you most want to write."

Through that process of reading and trying to understand, I learned a lot about what this man does. He works on billion dollar equipment headed for Mars. For years, his main job has been vibration testing. That would frighten the daylights out of me, to go vibrating a billion dollar piece of equipment, just to find how far I could shake it before I wrecked it! Don't give me *that* job! Nevertheless, I learned something interesting through reading his manuscript.

I had a very different experience with another friend's book, *The Spiritual Danger of Doing Good*. When Peter Greer asked me to pre-read his manuscript, I found myself fascinated by his treatment of the subject. I subsequently wrote a really positive endorsement for him. These two books discuss completely dissimilar ideas and were written for totally different audiences; they are nothing alike. But I gained something from reading both.

I read more than books, of course. Last night I was reading *Time* magazine. Something intrigued me and I clipped out two pages. At the moment, I don't even remember the topic; that's not important. But I've trained myself to say, "Hmm, that interests me. I don't have time to get to it right now, but I don't want to leave it in there, either, because I'll throw it away and won't remember to go after it." So I clipped out the article, put it with my other things, and I'll come back to it when I have some time to really dig in.

Every day I look forward to what I might learn from my observations, conversations, and the printed word. I enjoy nothing more than to sit around the dining room table or in my library, discussing and learning about every topic imaginable. At the end of every day, I ask myself, "What did I receive and how did I grow?" Learning in this way is one way to attain personal authenticity.

Become a Creative Listener

If you really want to feed your curiosity, then recognize that conversation is really much more about listening than it is about talking. Many of us spend so much time talking that we rarely take the time to truly listen. Yet by listening and actively engaging in the listening process—what I call "creative listening"—I learn so much more. Through creative listening, I'm better able to accomplish my critical tasks and I greatly increase my ability to pass along the things I've learned.

Becoming a creative listener is not easy; it takes a lot of work. It requires asking clarifying questions inappropriate to the flow of the dialogue. Because I'm curious about others, about what they know and what I can learn from them, I must give them permission to push back on my questions, however appropriate I think them to be. This may not always feel comfortable, but if I'm truly about learning, then I want them to have that right to push back. At the same time, we need to take risks and go places where almost certainly it may not feel comfortable. As we speak and listen, we need to remain vulnerable; and as we do so, the person we're spending time with tends to become far more vulnerable in turn.

As the adage says, it takes much more energy to dig out of a hole than to work on level ground. Creative listening often provides the extra energy required to help someone out of that hole. Most of the people I spend time with already have the ability and the knowledge to solve their own problems, but in many cases, they have to overcome a good deal of unlevel ground. Creative listening often gives the two of us the energy required to dig out of the hole, and so become all that we can be.

In other words, this creative listening process helps me to become a problem solver, not merely a problem identifier. As I ask clarifying questions as a part of the creative listening experience, I help the person to better see the available options and solutions. I usually don't have more answers than the person; most often, the person already knows the answers, but just hasn't realized it.

I once had a conversation with an exec in which I kept asking questions, listened carefully to the man's responses, and then asked more questions. By the end of our conversation, the exec came to a firm conclusion about what he needed to do. He smiled and then said to me, "Greg, you knew all the time that this is where I needed to go, didn't you? You knew, but you didn't tell me. You wanted me to find out for myself."

To be actively engaged with creative listing does not mean, of course, that we're unaware of what else is going on around us. The ability to multitask is critical to one's ability to understand and to grow in awareness. And again, "awareness" is our primary goal. Through creative listening, we seek to understand; and by understanding, we take another step toward greater achievement and fulfillment.

Wide Beam, not Narrow Beam

As we feed our curiosity and make room for our inquisitiveness, we begin to understand the crucial importance of taking the long view of life. Many people live in a very narrow, shortsighted world. My experience tells me that in most cases, these people have not taken the time to learn broadly.

I occasionally get the opportunity to speak at a number of universities, to undergraduate and graduate students as well as to faculty members. In many cases, I speak with Ph.D.s and post-Ph.D. scholars. I have a simple message for them: "You need to become broader in your experience and knowledge base and to further develop your integrated critical thinking skills."

While it is obviously important for them to grow deep in their field of expertise, many of them readily admit a lack of understanding regarding fields outside of their primary focus. In many cases, they don't see the need to have a wide focus rather than a narrow one.

As we converse, however, it quickly becomes clear that many of them are doing research that requires them to submit requests for outside funding. This funding, it turns out, more often than not comes from individuals who do not understand the expertise of the particular researcher. So who gets funded? Those researchers who nurture a broader array of interests—interests that might intrigue those who authorized the grants—are many times more likely to receive funding.

The irony is that educators, who often speak of the necessity of acquiring knowledge, themselves often have a very narrow knowledge base. I have tried to stress that increased inquisitiveness, on a broad basis, will help them to achieve greater results. "We must train ourselves to see things that others don't," I say. "We must work to achieve a heightened sense of awareness that can take us to another level of learning and understanding."

Outside of academia, many of the Type A personalities I regularly deal with describe themselves as very inquisitive—but I notice they seem inquisitive only about their particular line of thinking, their particular line of expertise, or their specific business. They're narrow beam as opposed to wide beam. Most of them want to know why it's important to read about quantum mechanics or the spiritual danger of doing good.

To them I may say, "Let's say that you have to make a big presentation to a potential client, a very big and important client. You know your stuff inside and out, everything about it. Any kind of question, you can answer. But while you may understand *yourself*, what you really have to understand is the *other* person. And that other person is not you. If you don't understand that person, you may never get the chance to make a successful pitch. And even if you get to make the pitch, the other person may never hear it. Why not? Because you're making the pitch to you rather than to *them*."

I let them chew on that a while, and then I'll conclude, "If you're really interested in understanding the person you're pitching, then you had better be curious about them and their organization."

My experience tells me that if I can find a personal connection with someone, many times I can more easily have the crucial business conversation. That's why when I enter someone's office, I want to know what's in there. What does the office tell me about that person? I do that anywhere I go, even in taxicabs.

Years ago I got in a taxi in San Antonio with a couple of business friends. Whenever I get in a cab, I always look for the driver's nametag. If it looks like a name from overseas, I say, "Tell me about how you wound up here. Why did you come?"

That day, I learned all kinds of interesting things about the driver. I heard about his native country, his wife, his children, and his hopes and aspirations. After the conversation, my two business friends asked, "Greg, why do you do that? You know we were getting out of here in ten minutes. You'll never see him again."

"I know," I replied. "But I've learned something about somebody's story that I find really intriguing." It ended up being a real example to these guys, both of whom are significant leaders. If we train ourselves to be curious about the cab guy, then we're naturally geared up to do the same thing with others who might hold the key to something we really want to do in business. Once curiosity becomes a part of you, it applies in ways and in situations you can never anticipate.

Most business leaders are very deep in one very narrow channel, and they look for the answers to all their problems in that single channel—missing the fact that the whole, wide world is "out there." Curiosity urges us to observe the world, to learn what it might be able to teach us. Not everything we observe teaches us something "practical," of course. But everything we learn is intriguing. And intriguing things have a way of coming back to enrich us later on in ways we simply can't anticipate.

Unexpected Help

Corporations of all sizes today are recognizing that their continued success depends on creativity and innovation. Curiosity lies at the heart of both. The very essence of creativity is combining two or more apparently unrelated things in a helpful, new way—and that takes inquisitiveness, a generic curiosity about the world around you.

The catch is, we never know ahead of time that what we're learning here may hook up in some surprising way with what we learned over there. We never know when we might find an application that integrates the two in some unexpected, profitable way.

When I meet individuals who consider broad curiosity a waste of time, I sometimes say, "You know what? You may think you don't need to be curious. And you may think your career will be just fine without it. But someday, you'll run up against something that will retard or even freeze your career path, something you're simply not prepared to handle. Without curiosity, you'll *never* handle it. I can't tell you how many times I've seen some 'useless' idea become invaluable."

I've met some individuals whom I might term "professionally autistic." They're hyper-focused on some small piece of reality and they live and die in that little box. I don't know that any of them seem very happy or satisfied; they usually have some significant glitch in their lives. And so they work harder. And they work harder. And they work harder. They think, *If I just work harder, then I'll be satisfied.* They never grasp that by becoming more curious about the world around them, they might be able to learn *more* and work *less* and so enjoy greater satisfaction in life.

When I first started working with "Shirley," she was very good at what she did, but in a relatively narrow box. And then one day she started to dream about climbing out of the box. At first, she didn't understand the necessity of becoming naturally curious if she was to move outside her self-imposed world. We spent many hours talking through the issue.

"If you want to go there, Shirley," I told her, "you need to be interested about who your clients are and what they're all about, and not just in the narrow sense you're used to. You want to work with all kinds of businesses, right? You need to get to know, not just individuals, but the 'personalities' of whole companies. That takes curiosity, a broad kind of inquisitiveness."

Today, most of Shirley's income comes from the wider business world, not from her former clientele. She's had to adapt and learn and be curious about many things, because what she'd always done could not have taken her to where she is.

Simply being in an unfamiliar environment can make us acutely sensitive to unusual ideas and processes and "stuff" that would never find a place in a more familiar environment. Without warning, we see that one thing we never imagined was there. We never could have predicted it would be there, but there it is—and all of a sudden, some potent new ideas start clicking in our head, with the power to solve some persistent or difficult problem.

It Makes You a Better Human

Beyond all of this, inquisitiveness simply makes you a better human being. You don't become inquisitive merely because you hope to get something "big" out of it. This is no mercenary enterprise. You feed your curiosity because at the end of the day, you'll be able to say, "I learned something really new and different today that I wouldn't otherwise have learned. And that has made me a better human being."

Not long ago, the pastor of a large evangelical church had to leave his post after a very public moral lapse. He'd also served as the president of an influential national association. I remember reading how someone looked at his personal library afterwards, and discovered that all of his books had to do with management and leadership. He had no books about anything else.

It made me wonder. What if he had developed a curiosity about other things? What if he had nurtured an expansive inquisitiveness about issues outside of his narrow interest? Could that have helped in some way, maybe delivered him from the boredom that usually comes from remaining hyper-focused on one particular concern for a long time? I suppose we'll never know.

When you train yourself to be curious, it's as though you gain 180 degree vision, enabling you to intentionally see everything around you. You never know what you're going to learn—but almost always, it helps you to become a better person. The principle of inquisitiveness is the foundational block for becoming all that you can be.

Curiosity Is Its Own Reward

Much of curiosity and inquisitiveness isn't about productivity at all. We value it simply because we want to know something we currently don't know. We see something interesting and we decide to learn about it, and so we become broader and deeper as we gain a larger sense of things. In so doing, we become both more interested persons and more interesting individuals.

A few years ago, someone asked if I had time to take John Stott, the late English theologian, out on my boat to Catalina Island. John wanted to see some eagles. I didn't even know eagles lived on Catalina Island, so I learned something just by entertaining the request. I agreed, and on the day of the expedition, I said to my captain, "This guy wants to see eagles."

"I know right where they are," he said.

As we approached Catalina Island, about halfway between its two towns, a pair of eagles flew directly by us. And then they soared up to the cliffs and landed in their nest. John watched them for about ten minutes through his binoculars and then said, "Okay, I'm done. We can go back." That also intrigued me. It turned out John was a great birdwatcher.

As we talked, I learned that John had traveled the world seeking out literally thousands of different birds, recording every sighting. When we returned to the Newport Beach harbor, John very casually said, "That bird doesn't belong here."

"What do you mean?" I asked.

"That bird is only in Australia and New Zealand," he insisted.

"But it's here," I replied. "What do you mean, it doesn't belong here?"

The captain overheard our conversation and chimed in: "Yeah, everybody in the harbor knows that bird. Somebody brought it from Australia or New Zealand, didn't want it, and then let it out."

All of those facts intrigued me, despite the odd mixture of information. What do you do with random facts learned by exercising curiosity? I don't know. But they often generate conversations in unpredictable ways.

At the end of our trip, John gave me a devotional book on birds, featuring his own photography. To this day, I have a great memento of taking John Stott on an impromptu bird watching trip.

Later at dinner, we enjoyed three solid hours of great conversation. I didn't know John well and had never met him before that day. But I had read something of his theological interests. One in particular had sparked my curiosity. So I took a risk and said, "John, please tell me a little about your annihilation theory."

I heard some gulps, but why not ask the question? It might be the only chance I'd have to ask the man about something that interested me.

So we'd looked at birds and talked about them, and now we discussed annihilation theory. My mind wanted to work on both fronts. I love the ocean. I love theology. I'd learned some things about birds, which is not a big love of mine, but it was fun to learn something new. And now I had the chance to learn something from a man of wisdom regarding a perspective quite different from most in the evangelical community. What kind of day is that? It was a great day—and all because of being curious and inquisitive and desiring to learn new things.

Somebody might ask, "But what if knowing that stuff never benefits you in a practical sense?" It's irrelevant. The new knowledge benefits the moment. I don't try to bring meaning to everything in the moment. I just want to enjoy the pureness of seeing, observing, learning and being curious about the world around me.

One time during a trip to Israel, while sitting in a restaurant, Antje and I spotted a couple of men wearing big, fur square hats. The hats didn't seem to quite fit the surroundings, so I decided to investigate. I went over to the men, introduced myself, and said, "I'm very curious to understand the meaning behind what you're wearing."

The men graciously explained why they wore the hats and told me they felt glad I had taken the time to ask the question. They were members of a Polish-Jewish sect that used the hats to remember their ancestors coming out of Egypt, wearing nothing but the clothes on their back. One man came from London, the other from Brooklyn. The next morning, we saw them again and we had another delightful conversation. That's how life changes.

Most of the cool new things you learn may never find some "practical" use in your business. But some will. And you never know ahead of time which will and which won't. And please hear me when I say, *it doesn't make any difference.* Learning new things through exercising your curiosity is its own reward.

An acquaintance of mine has worked for years with engineers. He once told me, "As I reflect on the engineering types I've worked with in leadership, I realize that, in general, they're very narrowly curious around their specific area of expertise. They're not broadly curious. And so they actually make poor leaders, because they think in very constricted, predictable ways. They're interested only in those things that they can see will have some practical application. And if they don't see a practical application, they screen it out."

Anyone can learn to be broadly curious. But first they have to come to believe that there's more outside of themselves, interesting things that they would like to discover and explore.

The Power of "I Don't Know"

Many people have a great reluctance to say, "I don't know." Yet this process of being inquisitive is the *perfect* time to say, "I don't know, but I would like to know." If we can bring ourselves to the point of really desiring to acquire a greater breadth and depth of knowledge, then we quickly learn to welcome the discipline of saying, "I don't know." I've learned that such a discipline helps me to avoid negative surprises.

A number of years ago, I was a partner with a well-regarded executive in a new business venture. Shortly after we began our partnership, my partner called to say that we had missed something important in the contract. We had overlooked a solvable problem, but the solution involved a significant amount of money. Immediately I asked for a meeting.

I told my partner that I didn't do well with surprises, particularly negative ones. In fact, I hate surprises. But I also had to admit that if I had exercised an appropriate amount of initial curiosity, we might have been able to avoid the surprise altogether. I thought we both needed to acknowledge that fact, so we could avoid such surprises in the future.

Do you know much about painting? I know a little more

now than I used to, mainly because my wife is an artist. But that doesn't mean I naturally understand all paintings.

"Las Meninas," a famous painting by Diego Velazquez, hangs in Madrid's Prado Museum. Experts around the world universally consider it a masterpiece. When I visited the Prado a few years ago, I wondered, *What accounts for the great beauty and intrigue of this painting?*

As I stood in front of the painting for several minutes, pondering its beauty, I slowly began to understand what the artist had done. Velazquez used a mirror to change the entire perspective of his work. Observers see the King and Queen, the expected subjects of the portrait, only in the mirror on the far wall. The painting really focuses on the painter himself. If I had approached the painting without curiosity, without a sense of inquisitiveness—if I had failed to say, "I don't know, but I'd like to know"—I would have missed one of the most unique and potent works of art in the world. And what a shame that would have been!

It's a Choice

Any of us can learn to become inquisitive, as a matter of habit. It simply takes a choice. I learned a lot of this because I *chose* to. I *chose* to become curious. I chose to become inquisitive. You can, too. Just try it for a while. Become curious. Let it be in you. Become aware. And as you're aware, feel what happens inside.

Almost without exception, our bodies respond in positive ways when we allow our curiosity to push us learn new things. We get an "endorphin rush" that gives us a good feeling, a burst of exhilaration.

Anyone can learn to embrace this kind of curiosity. I have a friend with two young daughters, ages eight and six. Sometimes he'll suggest the older one try something new, and she'll almost automatically reply, "Oh, I don't want to do that." Her dad will reply, "How do you know you don't want to do that, if you've never done it before?" Most of the time, she'll acquiesce at some point and try the new thing. And almost always, he tells me, she says excitedly, "Hey, that was a lot of fun!" She's learning to choose to embrace a broad kind of curiosity.

The beauty of inquisitiveness is that it's something that we choose and want to do, rather than being told we have to do it. I hope you'll agree and then choose to feed your own curiosity. You won't be disappointed.

Don't Take It Too Far

I can be hypersensitive. A friend had the courage to point that out to me a few years ago. I can have a tendency to take my curiosity so far that I begin to misinterpret things I see or hear. I had to learn to back off of that kind of self-focused curiosity, to avoid becoming so hypersensitive that I let it control me. Most often it's best just to observe, to listen, and then let it go at that.

It's certainly possible to become so curious about everything that you allow a hypersensitivity to inappropriately start controlling you. *I wonder what he meant by that? Was she insinuating something about me? Do they think I'm out of my league?* A healthy kind of curiosity lets new information and experiences flow naturally into our lives, in ways that enhance who we are and what we do.

The mother of a friend of mine had a tendency in this unhelpful direction. She used to occasionally play the piano in a small church in a tiny community. She and her husband had retired to this little town and loved it. As a frequent volunteer, she had a small "mailbox" at the church where people could drop off sheet music, notes, etc. After she played the piano one Sunday, someone left a little Tic-Tac in her box. And then she started obsessing about it. *Do I have bad breath? Who thinks I have bad breath? Does everyone in the church think I have a problem with bad breath?* She anxiously mentioned the Tic-Tac to a friend, who said, "What are you talking about? Nobody thinks you have bad breath! Just stop it, will you?"

Sometimes, a Tic-Tac is just a Tic-Tac. Sometimes, it means nothing except that someone missed the wastebasket.

The danger of getting hyper-curious is that we can allow it to get in the way of actually observing what we need to see. While we sit there worrying about who thinks we have bad breath, we miss the clues sent off by someone sitting right next to us, an individual in need who could really use our help.

As I mentioned earlier, I wrestled competitively in college, and over the years I've used the analogy of being a wrestler in a tournament. On the day of a tournament, a wrestler might have four or five matches, with one hour of rest between matches. I learned that whether I won or lost, I could not dwell too long on any prior match. I had to ask simple questions: "What did I do well? What did I do poorly? What could I have done better?" Regardless of my answers, I knew that the next wrestler would present a challenge quite different from the one I just faced.

So here's the principle: While we need to deeply understand each of our experiences, we must not obsess on any of them. We can't allow ourselves to get hypersensitive. Instead, we must turn our energy toward the future and apply the lessons we've learned in a constructive way. In other words, we consciously orient our curiosity more toward the future than to the past.

The Great Benefits of Inquisitiveness

Effective leaders enter into every situation with a healthy dose of curiosity. Since they have a broad desire to learn, they observe carefully and develop the knack of asking good questions—and their inquisitiveness produces a host of significant benefits. Consider just a few of them. Inquisitiveness . . . .

- Enables leaders to interact effectively with a wide variety of people. Being curious and genuinely interested in another person, for example, tends to ease that person's level of discomfort. Have you ever felt uneasy at a cocktail party when someone began talking to you, but you noticed his eyes continuing to scour the crowd? The whole encounter felt feigned, pretend. And sure enough, as soon as he found someone "more interesting," he left. Genuine curiosity, true inquisitiveness, is about personal growth, both personally and professionally. It therefore never has to feign interest, because that interest is real, which helps people to relax.

- Allows leaders to see things others don't, and thereby enables them to take advantage of excellent opportunities that others miss.
- Allows leaders to be vision casters, to know what it means to have a clear, simple, repetitive focus on where the organization is going and why.
- Helps leaders to face into reality, even an ugly reality. In a number of books and other writings, my friends, Drs. Henry Cloud and John Townsend, address the need to face into our reality. Learning and growing through being inquisitive is one method of facing into our reality. It may not reveal a pretty picture, but even so, it helps us as leaders to become fully aware of the important issues we face, which may include dealing with our own low self-esteem and low self-confidence. My work over many years with many leaders has shown me that, almost universally, significant leaders suffer from low self-esteem and low self-confidence (even though it often gets masked by many kinds of activities). Through the process of inquisitiveness, however, we can begin to develop the ability to enter our worlds in a far more self-confident way.
- Gives leaders a long view of life in a shortsighted world, leading to a breadth of learning that helps them to resist unrealistic expectations.
- Helps leaders to act more responsibly toward people and

to make more responsible decisions. I know what I don't know, and therefore I am careful not to judge a situation in advance. I try to listen carefully to hear what someone is really saying, beyond the mere words. Because I have listened carefully and tried to understand the underlying meaning, I can act more responsibly both relative to the other person and to decisions yet to be made.

- Empowers leaders to think more into the future, which helps them to become more competitive and enables them to act in a more intelligent and less defensive way. Many people live their lives totally in the present moment and take very little time to ponder the future. The problem is, this mode of living often leaves them surprised by the very future that they could have anticipated, at least to some degree.

- Gives leaders an element of control they would otherwise lack. When you have a greater depth and breadth of knowledge at your disposal, you increase your ability to influence wise decision-making.

- Helps leaders to better understand their core giftedness and personal history, identify their true passions, see where they can make a difference and what challenges remain to be solved.

- Helps leaders to understand what they fear and why they fear it, and so to identify healthy fear as opposed to unhealthy fear.

- Permits leaders to cross-fertilize their ideas with the ideas of others, which tends to lead to affirming others, which tends to encourage those others to trust them and look to them for help and growth.

- Equips leaders to become problem solvers, not merely problem identifiers.

- Enables leaders to become healthy skeptics. Harve Chrouser was one of my mentors during my college years. Harve believed in being in the thick of things. He believed in giving people lots of authority and responsibility, but he also strongly believed in the wisdom of the adage, "You don't get what you expect; you get what you inspect." I believe this conviction came from both his military service and his days as a college coach. On the one hand, Harve desperately wanted people to learn and to grow, so he constantly encouraged them. On the other hand, he became very engaged to make sure things happened in the way that he expected them to happen. He was a very curious man, never at a loss for ideas, never at a loss to try to understand new dynamics in ways that would make a positive difference.

• Teaches leaders to avoid unrealistic expectations. Just about the time I think I've "learned it all," I discover that I have many more things to learn. A breadth of learning helps me to recognize how much I don't know and so reduces foolish expectations.

Curiosity is one of those gifts that just keeps on giving. Make sure you make yourself ready to receive everything it wants to give you.

Not All Who Wander Are Lost

When Frank Lloyd Wright was little, he visited his uncle's Vermont farm during the winter. The snow had fallen thick, covering the farm in a frozen mantle of white. When Frank's uncle had to get a chore done in a barn several hundred yards away from the house, he invited Frank to join him. The man made a beeline for the barn, using his thick legs to plow through the deep snow. Meanwhile, Frank wandered over here to look at a bird, and over there to look at a tree, and all over the property.

When the uncle reached his destination and completed his task, he said, "Frank, come here for a moment. I want to tell you something." When Frank joined him, he said, "Take a look at our paths."

So Frank looked. The uncle's path went straight as an arrow to his target, while Frank's wandered over hill and dale.

"What does that tell you?" the uncle asked. He intended to teach Frank that when you have a job to do, you cut out all the side excursions and focus on the task. He wanted Frank to see that in his meandering all over the farm, he had wasted all kinds of energy.

At the time, Frank kept silent; but in later years, he would tell audiences, "I'll tell you what I learned that day. I learned that I never wanted to be as single-minded as my uncle and so miss so much of life." That single sentence explains why he ended up becoming Frank Lloyd Wright, one of the most creative architects in history.

Don't miss out on life. Choose curiosity. Choose inquisitiveness. And see what it can help you to become.

Intentionality

*The Conscious Act of Focusing
Your Energies to Know More*

A business acquaintance of mine served as a senior official in the university system of South Vietnam prior to its fall to the North Vietnamese. When the Americans left and the South got overrun, the new regime considered him a problem because of his leadership role. His pregnant wife and his child managed to escape to Thailand, her birthplace. He landed in prison.

But he refused to stay imprisoned. He plotted to find a way to escape and to reunite with his family. In time, he did manage to escape, but only to get quickly recaptured. As punishment, his guards buried him up to his neck for an extended time. He barely survived.

As he regained some of his strength, he escaped a second time, only to be recaptured again. Nevertheless, he remained firm in his resolve to be reunited with his family, and in time he made a third attempt, this one also unsuccessful. On his fourth attempt he made it as far as Cambodia, but he was recaptured and imprisoned again. He continued this cycle until, on his fifth try, he made a clean escape. He and some others stole a skiff and headed to Thailand. This time, after a long and nerve-wracking sea crossing, he found his family. An amazing reunion followed.

I had one just question for him: "What kept you motivated?"

His reply clearly revealed the focus of this chapter, *intentionality*. "I loved and wanted to see my wife and children again," he declared, "and I would do whatever it took to make that happen."

What Is Intentionality?

Intentionality is a stretching beyond to know more because you have a sense that there is more to know. It is the conscious intent to observe, ask questions and learn from whatever you see, hear, and read, remaining alert to learn in every possible way.

Intentionality involves a leader's intensity, will, and thoughts, aimed at a process of deeper understanding that takes both work and time. Intentionality is designed to know the specifics of the circumstances in which we find ourselves. It goes beyond our natural curiosity.

Intentionality, not unlike inquisitiveness, is an intellectual exercise. It helps us to focus on priorities (instead of mere demands) and helps us to better understand the choices in front of us as we take the time to actively, deeply and deliberately understand what we're facing.

The Funnel

When we're intentional, we don't let life "just happen." While part of inquisitiveness lets things just flow to us, intentionality takes the awareness we gain from our curiosity and uses a large funnel, as it were, to reduce the gallons of data. We dig at something with vigor, determined to get at the core of it. We want to uncover the heart of it, understand it in its full depth.

At this point, of course, our intentionality still just fills our minds with more data, more information. We observe. We ask clarifying questions. We dig at the problem one way, and then we dig at it from another direction.

Suppose someone tells me something alarming (or intriguing). I intentionally seek out someone more informed than I am and say, "Help me to understand. Give me some more information." Or I'll do some reading. Or I'll find another source of information that fills in the gaps generated by my inquisitiveness. I intentionally bring my funnel to the issue and use it to screen out the extraneous and reveal the significant.

My co-author, Steve Halliday, got his Ph.D. in communication a few years ago. In a "history of communication" class, he had to do a minor paper on a Christian communicator. His prof didn't care who the person was or when in history he or she lived. Steve wanted to get acquainted with someone he knew nothing about, so first he had to get out his wide-mouth funnel and look everywhere, just to see what came up. Eventually he bumped into a sixth century leader named Columcille, and soon he said, "That's my guy." At that point, he intentionally traded his wide-mouth funnel for a narrow funnel that sharply focused his attention on his new target. This funnel approach allowed him to go from lots of options to just one.

If we make that same application to all sorts of issues in our lives, we are much less likely to make decisions on partial information or on a whim, because we've intentionally determined to discover, "what else?"

Living Superficially

A lot of people live in a very superficial world, nearly devoid of funnels. Even if they're curious, even if they're inquisitive, they don't go deep enough. They live superficially. I try to help them understand that the world can be so much more interesting when we go deeper.

If we make decisions from a superficial point of view, we probably won't make decisions as good as if we were more intentional. We need to ask, "What's the rest of the story? What don't I know that I need to know?" Your intentionality should drive you deep into the areas you consider important.

Back in 2012, Howard Schultz wrote a book titled *Onward*, describing what happened behind the scenes as he helped to build Starbucks. After building the company, he basically said, "I've had enough. I'm walking away," at which point the company brought in a new CEO to run things. Soon afterward, however, the business started to tail off and the board brought Howard back. His book details example after example of how he or someone close to him would express some interesting idea, to which he always insisted, "We need to find out more about that." That's intentionality. To this day, when you visit Starbucks you see it intentionally making changes, trying new things. Right now it's attempting to figure out if some stores should serve alcohol. The company researches even the type of equipment it uses and the sort of aroma its stores create. The kind of intentionality that goes into designing a Starbucks store is simply phenomenal.

Of course, visitors to Starbucks seldom fully recognize the depth of detail that *somebody* went to in order to think through the whole consumer experience. Starbucks wants that experience not only pleasant, but one that earns a rabid repeat business.

On the opposite end of the spectrum, I think of a story decades old. Back in the mid-80s, when SAS Airlines was in decline, Jan Carlzon came in as the new CEO. He decided to empower his frontline employees to make any customer service decision. He thought this would make his customers happy and keep them coming back. It seemed to work, and he wrote a book about the strategy called *Moments of Truth*.

The problem with the idea, from my perspective, was that it didn't appear to dig deep enough. It seemed to me like a very top-level decision that lacked enough intentionality to fully understand the core dynamics of the problem. So for a few years, I tracked the airline's performance, even acquiring the company's annual report. I wanted to compare and contrast the airline's before-and-after fortunes. I wanted to intentionally understand, "Did this work?"

The book took off and became a worldwide phenomenon, with a celebrated focus on empowering employees to take care of customers. Three years later, however, in the airline's annual report, Carlson admitted, to his credit, that he needed to change his policy. While SAS had good intentions, and while it had enjoyed a short-term spike in business performance, it then suffered a rapid decline—to levels below where it had started before the implementation of the policy.

What had happened? Without the proper exercise of corporate judgment, customers had begun to ask for *and get* whatever they wanted, costing the company a fortune. It turned out that frontline people simply didn't have the skills or experience required to make the kind of calls they'd been empowered to make. And the company suffered.

Carlson wisely brought balance to his initiative. He became more intentional. He asked, "What must we do to take care of our customer, while protecting our bottom line?"

In the meantime, however, a lot of companies decided to follow the advice of his book, without taking the time to go deep, like Carlson himself eventually did. Many businesses just read the book and said, "This is what we need to do," long after he'd revised his policy. You can imagine what happened. I learned a lot by tracking that situation. I saw clearly the importance of intentionality for any organization or business.

The same thing holds true for churches. Many years ago, Willow Creek Community Church near Chicago pioneered a "seeker-friendly" initiative that caught the fancy of congregations all over the world. But not long ago, Bill Hybels, the pastor, created a bit of stir by admitting, "We made some mistakes. We neglected some elements of discipleship."

Even so, many churches continued to pursue the original template, without reference to the mid-course corrections. Again, a lack of intentionality, the failure to go deep, has caused problems for these churches, difficulties that they could have avoided.

You Don't Need to Know Everything

This focus on intentionality may sound as if I expect you to have unlimited knowledge. In fact, I believe no such thing. It's perfectly okay not to know the future or have all the answers. I wish I had learned earlier in my career that it's okay to say, "Sorry, I don't know." But in my own sense of needing to be valued, in those days I felt I had to have an answer for everything.

I don't. And neither do you.

My approach today is, "I don't know, but I want to know more." I intentionally focus on the fuzzy area in every way possible. This allows me to take a deep breath and to catch up while I listen creatively. I now see this exercise of intentionality as a challenge to grow. It is not a negative, unless we make it so. It does, however, require us to dig deep, to go where we may not initially want to go.

An executive I worked with had tried to work with a number of prior coaches, but none of them lasted long. When things got tough, he bailed. He told me that, many times, the coach had bailed. While he may have been right, I began to see that, more likely, his own inability to see inside of himself became so discouraging for both parties that the process of learning just stopped.

Early on in our relationship, this executive challenged me on some of my thinking. I sensed it was a test. I told him that as long as he was prepared to remain in the arena, I would be there, battling it out with him. I wanted both of us to become better. I didn't need to know everything, and he didn't, either. But we both needed to intentionally work to get better.

Understand People at Their Core

In this process of going deep and caring and wondering, we begin to develop a significant connection with the people we've been called to lead. Through this process, we begin to understand our people at their core.

Some time ago, a professional with whom I had not spoken

in many years approached me through LinkedIn™ to connect. In her first communication, she indicated that I had said something to her decades before that influenced her life and ultimately the lives of her children. I had no recollection of the encounter.

In a return e-mail, I asked if she would be so kind as to remind me of what I had said. The following is the essence of the story.

We had hired her as an architect responsible for the design of storefronts to be added to a major new mall in one of our primary cities. I had come for a visit from corporate, and she felt very uncertain about her status. As we walked down the main courtyard, she felt very frazzled, but told me that I kept assuring her it would all work out and we would make the opening date. She confessed to me a great anxiety about making the wrong decision.

"If your decision costs the company half a million dollars, but we still make a million dollars, we'll be a success," she said I told her. "If at the end of the day, your decision turns out to be not a good one, we will sit down and discuss what we learned. As long as you made the decision wholeheartedly, believing it to be a good one, and you learn from that experience, I will have your back." She told me that I paused and then added, "But if you make the same decision again and do not learn from that mistake, then we will part company."

In this case, my intentionality was about giving her the kind of support that allowed her to take risks so she might achieve greater-than-expected results. I'm happy to say it worked—not only in the short run, but also in the long run of her life.

Plan for the Unplanned

It's important to intentionally plan for the unplanned. When I look at my calendar, I often see every day totally booked. For every minute, I know the schedule—but too often, I haven't planned for the unplanned. I've not allowed space in my day and my life in which I can address the important but unexpected things that come up. So I've learned to try to schedule time for the unplanned.

If I take the long view, that means I don't need to have every answer for all things today. I can begin to have the freedom to explore what I don't know. Society has projected on leadership the need to have answers now, always now. By taking the long view, I realize that there are more things to learn that might broaden my capacity to make a significant difference in my world. When I began to exercise my leadership in this way, I started to realize that this new paradigm often created opportunities for better, more legitimate choices. That's what often flows from a wider knowledge base.

Through this process, we're always learning. We begin to understand what it means to anticipate, as well as to acknowledge what we don't know. Keeping our focus on expanded learning and intentionally putting ourselves in the shoes of those around us begins to take us to a new depth. This doesn't mean we stop focusing on important areas of achievement; rather, based on our prior experience, it means becoming more aware of what *might* happen and doing what we can to mitigate the unlovely aspects of any such possible scenario. We see doing good things ahead of us. We see new opportunities. And we prepare for them.

Take Steps, Not Leaps

We learn from the whole journey of life, not just from a particular point in time. I liken it to stair steps. We step up and find a flat step, which gives us a time to catch our breath. And then we step up again.

We don't need to take bounding leaps. We don't have to play Superman. A step at a time will do.

As we challenge ourselves with new information, we assess, we take it in, and then we take another step up. This is what life in leadership is all about: Learning, growing, learning, growing.

One step at a time.

Look for the Exception

Many times as leaders, we get caught up in the minutia. We get so involved in the details that we miss the most important things, those things that should become key areas of enlightenment for us.

I've learned to lead in many cases by looking for the exception. What doesn't fit? Why doesn't it fit? With the limited time we have to get involved in many aspects of leadership, if we concentrate on the exception, we can use our gifts at a higher margin. In finance, perhaps I look for expenditures out of the ordinary. For accounts receivable, perhaps I look for a spike or a dip, maybe a big customer not paying some significant bill.

We trust our people to do what they're supposed to do, yet we look for the exception. What is the outlier? In conversations with other leaders, I've seen that by leading by exception, we can often get to the heart of the matter much more quickly—and all without getting distracted by relatively less important matters. What doesn't fit? What's out of the ordinary?

Learn Through Failure

I recently heard from a former colleague who sent me this quote: "The most valuable thing you can make is a mistake—you can't learn anything from being perfect" (Adam Osborne). She told me that the quote reminded her of the importance of taking risks. By refusing to take risks, she said, she steals from herself the chance to make mistakes and thereby grow.

She went on to acknowledge having made a lot of mistakes during her career, but also indicated she didn't regret those mistakes, except when her actions may have inadvertently hurt someone.

I have learned to intentionally embrace failure, not only because I learn from it, but also because I think it helps me to avoid unwelcome surprises. And as I've said, I don't like unwelcome surprises. Not everyone has the same outlook.

I once asked a leader if he had ever failed. "No," he said, "I don't remember ever failing." I had the task of walking with him as he began to discover a number of failures in his life. It really wasn't that he hadn't failed; it was more that he had no ability to acknowledge it was okay to fail. And therefore, he'd never learned from his mistakes.

We don't set out to fail, of course. But we're foolish if we refuse to recognize that each of us fails many times each day; at least, we all fail to measure up to the standards we set for ourselves. Since I desire to seek out all kinds of learning opportunities, I want to recognize my failures so that I may minimize the impact of those failures. I also look forward to the new learning experiences yet to come.

The end of the world doesn't come through failure. It's one way I learn, especially to make sure I don't repeat the mistake. The Zamboni story reminds me of this.

By my mid-twenties, I was responsible for a portfolio of properties and for the people who worked there. That included a large facility with twin ice rinks. I didn't visit the facility every day, but I did go one day. I'm the boss, right? And I wanted to drive the Zamboni, the cool machine that resurfaces the ice.

So I watched what the driver did. And I asked him, "What do you need to do to operate this thing?" He told me, and I replied, "I think I can do that." So between periods of the hockey game, I went out to the Zamboni, climbed aboard, and started driving. As I looked behind me, I saw the blade wasn't shaving any ice, as it was supposed to. And the auger wasn't pulling up any ice. That really confused me; it wasn't supposed to happen.

The Zamboni has a crank that alters the angle of the blade. So I thought, *Well, maybe he just flattened it too much. If I just crank it a bit, then it will drop the angle and it will start shaving.* So I did that, but it still wouldn't work. So I cranked it a little more. Still nothing.

And then I thought, *Oh, yeah, I know what I'm supposed to do.*

I haven't engaged the hydraulic, which drops down the whole back end of the machine. And so I dropped the hydraulic, without first cranking the blade back up.

Ka-*boom!* The front end of the Zamboni immediately shot up. I came very close to severing the plastic pipes underneath the ice, the ones that freeze the water. Had I hit those pipes, we'd have lost the whole ice sheet. That would have been a *big* deal.

Okay, Boss. You're in front of thousands of people. You just did this crazy, stupid thing that you should never have done without practice. You can't point the finger at anybody else. You can't say, "Joe, why did you *do* that?"

It was all me.

And so the question is, what did I learn from that experience that I could apply to other areas of my life? How could I go forward and use it to my advantage in the future?

First, I had to admit that I'd pulled a boneheaded move. Nobody forced me. An immediate lesson came to mind: *Don't try something like that in public without first getting some practice.*

Second, I learned that because I can acknowledge my own failure, I can I give grace to others who mess up. And I can help them to never do it again.

A lot of organizations don't give a lot of grace, so a lot of their people are afraid ever to raise their hand. I want to change the structure of organizations so they embrace the power of grace that leads to learning and growing and becoming better. But it has to start somewhere, with somebody raising their hand and saying, "it was me."

Of all the things I ever shared about my failures at Coldwell Banker, the one thing most people remember is the Zamboni story. It said to everyone in the organization, "I make mistakes."

I can tell a lot of stories about my mistakes. I once hired a guy in Chicago at Homart Development Company. I moved him from Denver to serve as our vice president. A month later, I knew he wasn't going to make the cut. He wasn't the right guy. But I also knew it wasn't his fault. He was actually pretty talented and could do many things well, but he didn't have what we needed. I realized I hadn't done my work properly to understand his gifts versus our needs. The mistake had nothing to do with him.

And so I said to him, "We're going to have to let you go, but here's what we're going to do. We're going to really take care of you. We don't have any legal obligation to do so, but we're going to pay for the cost of relocating you again and moving you, if you need to move again. We're going to help you find a job. We're going to pay you for an extended period of time while we help you find other employment."

He was angry. His wife was angry. They had just moved their family and they didn't know what the future would hold for them. They didn't know anybody in their new situation. And of course, people in my own company went crazy. "You can't do this! You've got to give him six months." But it wasn't his problem, it was mine. At the same time, I had an obligation to do what was right for the company.

Six months later, I got a letter from the guy. He had moved to Indiana. "Greg," he said, "I can see I'm in a place where I really fit. I'm in the right place." So it worked out better for him in the long run. He would have been unhappy with us, and we would have been unhappy had he stayed.

Intentionally learn from your mistakes. And intentionally look for ways to use those mistakes to help both yourself and your people to grow.

The Benefits of Intentionality

As leaders intentionally focus their energies, they bring clarity and consistency to the challenges facing them. And that focused energy brings a host of important benefits.

1. *Push and pull*

    Intentionality enables leaders to learn which followers to push and which to pull—not an easy task. When I take the time to understand the breadth of the task in front of us, I can best determine which people in the organization need to be pushed and which who need to be pulled. I like to use the analogy of horse riding. Some horses respond best to pulling on the reins; others need to be prodded. In both cases, whether we push or pull, we reach the objective.

2. *Know the degree of risk*

Effective leaders must know the degree of risk appropriate to both individuals and to the organization. Because we have asked the right questions and have learned in the broadest possible way, we can take a reasoned approach to risk-taking. While some individuals don't identify themselves as risk takers, I contend that all leaders are risk takers, somehow or in some way. The question is, do we know how we are taking risks? Many times, the most risk-averse individuals, by virtue of that very aversion to risk, take the biggest risks of all—and they don't even know it until it's too late.

3. *Assimilate ideas, identify options*

The intellectual process of intentionality allows us to begin to assimilate ideas, concepts that for the moment don't need to be acted upon. Rather, we put them into our mental databank. The world of ideas and the ability to assimilate those ideas gives the leader greater opportunities to know options. Many times when I read books, I note in the margins the phrase, "yes/but." In nearly every case, the principle involves making sure that we are digging deeper with intentionality into the core issues, and not being superficial. I want to be myself, fully engaged, fully aware and fully intent on learning everything possible about the task in front of me. In intentionally going the direction I believe we need to go, nevertheless I must recognize that I may not have thought of everything. It therefore becomes my responsibility to continue to seek out more knowledge.

4.   *Minimize and mitigate fear*

Over my many decades in business, I've seen one consistent theme arise among leaders, one that no one wants to talk about: Fear. Fear paralyzes us. Along with fear comes a universal need for affirmation. The irony is that these two things, fear and affirmation, work in tandem. Very few leaders will acknowledge fear, yet when confronted in an appropriate way, most of them acknowledge a sense of fear about making a mistake (at the very least). When I as a leader seek to gain the greatest possible breadth of knowledge, there is less cause for fear. Still, most leaders spend little time doing the things necessary to minimize and mitigate the reasons for fear. Many of the executives I've worked with deal with this issue during negotiations. All leaders see themselves as competitors, and every competitor wants to win. Consequently, during negotiations of any decent size, there is always a good possibility that we will not win. I've learned to feel comfortable with that. If I can say I've done the best I possibly can, then I have little reason to fear.

5.   *Dig deep by asking good questions*

Much of intentionality is about asking questions, of all sorts. Those questions allow us to dig deep. Leaders are inquisitive, curious, and they want to know more. Questions are a great way to acquire the information we need. To succeed in the broadest possible sense means that we cannot stop asking questions. One of my favorite questions is, "Does that make sense?" I find that asking the question shows my intentionality to want to know and understand the person to whom I'm speaking. I want to make sure that my interpretation of what the person has said is, in fact, what that person meant. Only through proactive questioning can we get to the reality of the spoken words. The process of understanding takes both work and time.

6. *Refuse to quit*

   I played a number of sports in high school and college, but primarily I wrestled. I had done well in high school and earned a high winning percentage in college. Many years after college graduation, I met with two of my college wrestling buddies who were slightly older than I. One of them, a former national collegiate champion as well as an outstanding coach at major universities, told me. "Greg, you really weren't that good of a wrestler. You just didn't quit." Of course, his words initially delivered quite a blow to my pride. I'd always thought of myself as an outstanding wrestler. But I learned the lesson, and continue to learn it, that I must never quit. I keep learning and striving to be better. I keep finding new things that will help me do what I do, only more efficiently and more effectively. This intentional refusal to give up is one of the prime forces that moves us down the path of learning and growing toward becoming all we can be.

7. *Respectfully challenge the status quo*

   It's important not to settle for the status quo. I've always tried to tell the people I work with that I expect them to challenge my thinking, in an appropriate way. It wasn't good enough for me that I could challenge their thinking; I needed my thinking to be challenged as well. If the first time someone challenged my thinking, I berated them or put them down, I would only demonstrate that I was not serious about them challenging the status quo. It became important for me, as it is for all leaders, to become a model of wanting to know more. I do not have all the answers, but together, we know a lot and can do much more.

8. *Make good decisions on the best available information*

   I love boating and have boated most of my life. I love being on the ocean at night when it gets totally dark. I may see some stars or some part of the moon, but no land light.

Total darkness means total uncertainty as to the location of the shore, at least from a visual perspective. My senses tell me I need to turn the wheel in one direction, but the compass says, "Don't do that." Nevertheless, the pressure mounts to turn the wheel where my instincts want to go, not where my knowledge tells me to go. Through boating, I began to understand the need for balancing my feelings with realism. Am I ready to accept what the gauges, based on someone's prior knowledge, tell me to do? Or do I find it more compelling to do what I feel like doing? And if I go the direction I feel, am I prepared for the consequences, which could be disastrous? The principle here is making the best decisions based on the best information available. And on the boat, in total darkness, the best information available is what the compass tells me. On that boat, in the middle of the night, I can depend on my compass; but maybe it'd be even better if in addition to the compass, I had a GPS. That would give me two means of validating my decisions. Do they both tell me the same thing, or are they in conflict? By using validation, whether on the boat or in business, I can move toward a more satisfactory solution.

9. *Gain an alternate perspective*

    Early in my career, I managed small office buildings in the Chicago area. In the wintertime, that always meant snow. Because our own staff did the plowing, I wanted to understand the process of plowing the parking lots. So one day I went for a ride along. At some point, I asked if I could drive. Several things happened during that experience.

    First, I began to understand the reality of the actual work required, as well as the time required. It also afforded me significant time to converse with the employee as I tried to understand the plowing task. He told me he had never had that kind of experience, of being asked by a superior to be understood and to comment. It became a very enlightening time for me and an important time for him.

I did a number of things during the course of my experiment that would have upset me before the experiment, had the driver done them. But once I sat in the driver's seat, I began to understand that things sometimes happen that we don't fully control.

My experience illustrates that to be a truly effective leader, we must learn to look at the world through the eyes of another, from their perspective. We need to become so interested in knowing the other that we willingly put aside our prejudices in order to truly understand. But because we all have prejudices, this is no easy task. Still, the benefits of trying to understand a person in his or her totality, ultimately makes me a better person and allows me to function in a better way.

10. *Removes distractions*

The number of distractions in front of many executives keeps them from doing the things they most need to do. I recently spent time with the CEO of a very large organization. We discussed his calendar for the rest of the year and he described the many venues where he would have to give speeches. On further review, we recognized that many of the presentations were quite similar. By intentionally focusing on the reality of the man's schedule, we developed a new approach for him. He discovered that he did not need all of the preparation time he had assumed. Our conversation essentially focused on removing distractions. All leaders face an incredible amount of distraction. Many people want their time and attention. Yet if we are intentional and keep our focus on the most important things, we will face less distraction. We can intentionally focus our energies in those areas where we can make the most difference.

Quality Is Not a Given

All leaders want quality, but quality is not a given. Rather, quality comes from intentionally remaining focused on getting better.

Taking time to think and to reflect becomes critical as we input all kinds of new data. This process of intentionality helps us to determine what helps us to grow and to learn and to become all that we can be. This is an arduous task that takes dedication as well as patience. It takes having the ability to take the long view, that we still have more to learn. It requires us to bring clarity of expectation to those with whom we work and spend our lives.

As we show the depth of our care and interest in those with whom we spend time, however, we strengthen our relationships and so build a stronger company. This allows us to think beyond whatever decision currently confronts us and enables us instead to recognize that, no matter what, we'll still be in the arena for the next decision. We do not need to feel constrained by the immediate and the now.

Such is the power of intentionality.

Integration

Connecting the Dots

When I first arrived at Coldwell Banker, the company was losing $100 million annually on revenue of one billion dollars a year. The firm had brought me in as an outsider to help figure out a solution. So a lot of what I did for the first six months was to dig deep, trying to understand our unhealthy situation.

I knew going in that we had three main divisions, all with different business units and support staff. But I soon discovered that nobody really talked to each other. "How can we get these disparate pieces connected?" I asked myself. "How can we integrate these isolated business units?"

I couldn't just start making decisions on day one. That would be crazy. So I had to dig deep. I had to ask a lot of questions of many people. After I began getting a handle on things, it seemed obvious we had to bring together the different pieces of the company. We went looking for a property, eventually finding a vacant one large enough to house everyone.

At the time, I sat basically in the Number 2 chair. A seasoned veteran, far better known to the industry than I, would remain in the Number 1 chair. When he went back to Chicago to make a pitch to buy this $20 million dollar property, he immediately ran into some resistance. After his return, he shook his head and told me, "Greg, they said 'no.' They can't understand the reason for it."

I knew it really did make sense, but I also recognized we had not crafted together a clear strategy for explaining the purchase. "You and I both know we need to do this," I said. "Let's sit down and figure out how to explain it so that it makes sense to them. And then let's go back to Chicago and make a second pitch."

That's what we did, at the subsequent meeting, within ten minutes we had an agreement to spend $20 million dollars.

The problem? We hadn't done a good job of explaining what we had learned by going through the integration process. On our first attempt, we hadn't laid out a compelling picture of why and how this strategy would work. We just told the board, "We want to spend $20 million dollars to buy a building." They reacted very predictably: "Why? You'd have to break leases. There will be other expenses. You're already losing $100 million dollars. No." But once we could demonstrate how the decision made sense as a key part of an integrated strategy to get the company back to financial health, they quickly bought in.

What Is Integration?

Through integration, we take what we've learned via our inquisitiveness and intentionality and then begin the intellectual process of "connecting the dots." How does what we've observed and learned apply to where we are or what we need to do? Integration is a sense-making activity. We're still not "doing" anything. We're just trying to understand.

Integration asks us to consider how we might connect distinct pieces or elements and combine them into a new whole. How does what we've learned apply to what we're trying to be, as well as what we may attempt to do in the future? Integration is a form of adaptation. It is a way to take every aspect of information flow and use it to try to make helpful connections.

Integration also takes creativity. It moves beyond observation

to intellectually connecting things that may not seem connected. Organizations simply aren't efficient when they remain in
boxes. They become more efficient as we bring things together,
as we overlap.

Once we've completed one phase of integration, of course,
we may find that we don't like what we've learned. In that case,
we may choose to go back to learn more. Perhaps we've discovered that our knowledge base is quite large in one area but woe-
fully inadequate in another. If the pieces of information we've
just processed don't seem to fit together, then we ask, "What's
the missing piece?" That question drives us back into intentionality, to ferret out the missing piece.

Consistent success demands continual integration. I made
that discovery early in my career, when I found myself on the
fast track to corporate leadership. Before long, however, I became disenchanted with the company's leadership style, basically a "Father knows best" approach with a vertical, top-down
structure. Without having another job lined up, I left the firm.

A friend suggested I try real estate and arranged for me to
work in Chicago, where I attempted to lease office space downtown. I failed miserably. Only later did I discover that part of
my failure was an inability to integrate all the aspects of what it
would take for me to succeed.

Fortunately, my friend had a better handle on integration. He
saw my gifts and understood how I might most effectively apply
them. With his encouragement, I started over again in another
aspect of commercial real estate, which ultimately led to a successful career. The point here is that although it took someone
else to do the integration and see how it all fit together, that
integration still had to take place.

As I mentioned earlier, I love boats. But I learned quickly that
boats don't have brakes. I can put the boat in neutral, and it will
continue to move forward. Even when I put the boat in reverse,
it will continue to advance for a period of time. That means that

on the boat, I need to think ahead, anticipate, know what's coming. Only by integrating *my* knowledge of the speed of the boat, the movement of the waves, and the impact of the wind, can I understand when and how to dock my boat. Only when I know my boat—and each boat is different—can I best know how to remain in control of my nautical destiny.

What's the Need?

Despite its importance, integration is one of the more difficult and overlooked of the 5 I's. Many business people really don't see the need for integration; or at least, they don't grasp how it actually works. Many tend to see inquisitiveness, intentionality and integration as discrete tasks to be checked off a list: "Okay, got that one done. Yep, another one finished." They view them as separate, mostly unrelated jobs. But if we don't pay attention and see how the first two I's are integrated, we can run into significant problems or miss major opportunities.

At one point in my career, the CFO I worked with became a major roadblock to our progress. He prevented a lot of good deals from happening by spending too much time in analysis. He could always imagine a scenario in which something would go wrong. I finally went to him and said, "This process isn't working. You need to be integrated into the process in a different way. So let's make a deal. As long as our financials are within this group of boundaries, then there's no reason to block the deals. My group will be in the right place. And if we need to make further adjustments as we move forward, we can do so. But this will allow us to safely move ahead." We developed a better process by integrating the pieces of our operation, rather than keeping them in pieces.

Without integration, we suffer mental conflict where none needs to exist, since we compartmentalize our learning and so fail to get the maximum payoff from our hard-earned experience. Leaders who don't make the effort to fully integrate what they've learned with what they need to do often get stuck in a continuous data-gathering mode. Have you ever wondered why some leaders unconsciously tend to delay making tough, decisive decisions? This is why. They prefer deferral over the decisive, and continual data-gathering makes that preference possible.

Such a strategy reminds me of a scene at the pet store. Have you ever seen a hamster in a tumbler? The hamster never stops spinning inside his cage. He never stops running, yet never gets anywhere. The hamster keeps acquiring new information and recycling old information, without ever integrating what he's learned so that he can do something different or better. Although he sees the future right in front of him, the future never gets any closer, no matter how hard he runs.

If that's you on the tumbler, you really can get off. But it will take integration to do so.

Although integration is largely an intellectual exercise, instinct also plays a role. What does your gut tell you? Do you sense a "fit" between the disparate things you're investigating? What seems to be missing? Have you internalized so much that you've missed the obvious?

I once had a conversation with an author who wanted to make a fresh point in his new book. After listening to him talk, I suggested that his proposal seemed not unlike a three stranded rope; his problem was that he presented each strand as an end to itself.

As we discussed the integration concept and used the analogy of twisting the three individual strands into one new rope, his three separate points became much stronger. A single strand has nothing like the strength of a rope created by twisting together separate strands. It seems obvious—and yet, sometimes, it takes our gut to point out the fact to us.

Integration Once, Twice . . .

While our purchase of the $20 million building helped Coldwell Banker begin the integration process, we still had a lot more work to do. Our three major real estate business units—franchise, relocation and owned offices—for years had maintained their own headquarters. They felt angry that we forced them to abandon their independence. I told the three presidents of the business units, "Your offices will be right next to me."

You'd have thought I had just threatened to kill them.

"No, we need to be with our people!" they objected.

"Well," I insisted, "I need to be with my people. You're going to be right here, with me. When you learn to talk to each other and understand what each of you and your organizations does and needs, then we'll reconsider. But for now, you're going to be right here, because I want us to talk to each other." I didn't see how we could succeed without integrating our knowledge and interests.

The president of the franchise company lasted only about six months. He left because he couldn't handle the perception that he no longer seemed like the top dog in his world—although in reality, he still was. For several years during his tenure, the franchise company had put on big conferences featuring top speakers, but wouldn't allow our owned office real estate agents to attend, nor did our owned office company want them to. I said, "That's over, guys. And here's why."

Another integration issue involved the owned office business. Like the franchise company, it had its own identity and had told the other divisions, "Don't come near us." It had offices in the L.A. Metro and Seattle, for example, and declared, "Those areas are just for us. No franchising can be done there. That can be done only in secondary markets."

When I started looking at our locations, it didn't make sense. The owned office division covered only ten percent of some of its chosen markets, and one of them had lost a million dollars a year for ten years running. "We're going to do something different," I said. "Focus the owned business on where you can make money. We'll sell the rest of your locations around the country.

But there's a condition: You sell only to a company that will agree to become a franchisee."

The relocation division had its own issues. One branch wouldn't give the business it controlled to representatives of our owned division. Instead, it invited Remax or another competitor to step in. "No," I said, "that's not going to work. We may have to train some people how to take care of these customers, but the old approach stops now."

As a result of these changes, and others like them, our market share grew, even though our revenue shrank. For every dollar we used to get, now we were getting six cents—but our overhead nearly went away. Six years later, we were *making* $100 million on $700 million of revenue, as opposed to *losing* $100 million on $1 billion of revenue.

Eventually, our people started understanding that they really needed each other.

The presidents of our three business units ultimately became partners with me and my colleague. But at first, they refused even to talk business to one another. In time, they began to realize that talking helped us all. All three eventually became part of our profit making. At that point, we'd fully integrated everything.

This same kind of integration needs to happen in *every* group or organization. I know of a church, for example, that partnered for several years with a national ministry to mobilize its parishioners once a year to do some practical outreach into the community—cleaning schools, refurbishing parks, renovating community centers. The church closed down its services one Sunday a year and encouraged everyone to find an appropriate service project to join. Church leaders considered it a great success, and so it was.

But almost overlapping with the yearly outreach, the church also hosted an annual year-end celebration for a local school district, an event attended by several hundred parents and students, along with scores of faculty, school board members, city council officials, business executives and other community leaders. For some reason, the church didn't think to embrace the in-church event as it had embraced the outreach event. Church leaders didn't even tell the congregation it was hosting the thing, so almost no one from the church showed up to help, although their help would have been welcomed. The church spent hundreds of man hours each year and a lot of effort and money imploring its members to get out in the community to serve; but it basically ignored the one day a year when the community showed up in droves at its own facility—a classic integration problem.

I'm not picking on the church; the situation is fairly common. Most of us haven't figured out how to truly integrate disparate things, whether in our lives or businesses. We haven't learned to say, "Okay, if I'm already doing this over here, and I'm already doing that over there, is there a way to do something even better by bringing the two together?"

That's the challenge of integration, to look at apparently unrelated things and see if we can find a way to integrate them into a more successful whole. Is there a third or a fourth way to enhance our position, or at least provide a way for us to carefully consider an alternative?

Validating What We See
As we integrate, we need to make sure that what we think we see and understand is *actually* there. We need a variety of ways to validate our integration. Does our new understanding in fact sync up with reality?

If I'm going to properly integrate my new database, I need to recognize that I may not always have it quite right. This is the time to clarify and validate. I often ask the question, "Does this make sense?" Many times, that question allows me to do a better job of integrating all I've learned.

This is also a good time to use word pictures to paint for others the scene I'm seeing. As I paint the picture, I observe people's reactions. I watch their body language, as well as to listen to their tone. In this way, I work to validate (or invalidate) my attempts at integration. I try to make sure that what I believe to be true is, in fact, true (or recognize that I had it wrong). The goal here is to find a variety of ways to validate what we've done in our efforts at integration.

The Many Benefits of Integration

Successful integration not only helps us overall in the task of seeking to understand, but it also brings us several specific benefits. Integration . . . .

- *Encourages us to develop a discipline of time allocation.*
  If we remain only in the data-gathering mode and never try to understand what we've learned, we will waste a good deal of time. Integration reminds us to allocate our time so that we use some of it to gather data and some of it to analyze and integrate the data so gathered.

- *Balances our expectations of ourselves and of others.*
  How black and white is your world? Is there always clarity? Do you sometimes feel confused about the right answer to give or the best direction to take? When we integrate all that we know and learn, we're more likely to make decisions that recognize the "grayness" of life. Are there ethical rights and wrongs? Without question. Do they always seem clear to us? No.

  Sometimes we make decisions based on limited knowledge and so jump to conclusions before we have all the necessary data. And even when we arm ourselves with all the best data available, we still may not have enough information to know fully the best answer, even when we do the best job possible of integration.

  As we work from this realistic point of view, we are better able to balance our expectations, both of ourselves and of others. Most leaders I work with tend to have unrealistic expectations of themselves, as well as skewed expectations of their colleagues. By properly integrating who we are and what we know about each other, we have a better chance of achieving our objectives, even if our expectations look quite different from one another.

We have to be realistic. Although we may never obtain and integrate all the information needed to make a totally "right" decision, nevertheless, we have to wrestle through to the best choice possible. If we do not take the time to properly understand ourselves and our motivations, as well as those with whom we work—understanding that comes only through a thorough process of integration—we may miss (and probably will miss) our greatest opportunities for mutual success.

- *Gives us an alternative to the "no."*
My work with many kinds of leaders tells me that our first inclination is often to say "no." I suggest that we leaders must be prepared to go deeper, to seek out the true context of what someone is trying to tell us or ask us. If our typical first response is "no," we may miss out on good information. By automatically saying "no," instead of saying, "Help me to understand," we may lose the ability to acquire and integrate the very information that could ultimately lead to something far better.

- *Helps us to become competitor-aware, not competitor-driven.*
Most businesses have some kind of competitor. I believe it's important to become competitor-aware, not competitor-driven. By being competitor-aware, we assimilate as much information as we can about our competitor and integrate it with what we know about other competitors, as well as current market conditions. Following this true integration, we will have a much greater sense of the competition. When we become competitor-driven, however,

we are like a horse with blinders on. We see only that competitor and nothing else. And so we miss the rest of the world in which we're trying to operate.

- *Enables us to hire the right people.*

If we develop the necessary integrative skills, but lack a staff with those same skills, our organization will remain ill prepared for the challenges facing us. Therefore, it's important to hire people who share a desire for continuous learning, who have an ability to take what they've learned and fit it in to a broader model. Frankly, not everyone can do this.

A huge part of leadership, then, is about hiring the right people, as well as transitioning others out who lack the basic requirements. I'm a fan of hiring slow and firing fast. Our first goal has to be keeping the company solvent. While doing good things is great, if those good things kill the business, then who are we helping?

We avoid internal frustration, both personally and professionally, when we surround ourselves with those whose have a desire equal to our own to learn and grow and integrate.

In more cases than not, the success or failure of an organization comes back to the capacity of the individuals who make up the organization. Consequently, as I evaluate myself and others, I look at the task not unlike how I evaluate a financial investment. Can I get a greater return by hiring X than by hiring Y? Doing such an analysis forces me to understand not only what we do, but who we do it with. What are our capacities? Do we have the ability to accomplish the things we're committed to doing?

- *Makes effective goal-setting possible.*

Goal setting becomes an important part of what we do as we integrate all we've learned. When most people think of goal setting, they have in mind only the practical side of it; but effective goal setting is as much psychological as it is practical. If we think only about the practical applications and ignore the psychological, we may miss the greatest opportunity of goal setting of all. Integration that leads toward setting appropriate goals *stretches* us yet remains *achievable* for us, in both the practical and psychological senses.

To achieve the psychological goal, I must hear from my colleagues and coworkers. And to hear, I need to really *hear*. Truly hearing involves more than merely recognizing the words used; it requires getting behind the words. Do we take time to really hear what's being said to us? Do we refuse to assume that we understand, merely because we can parrot back the words?

- *Teaches us to be vulnerable.*

A number of years ago, a university professor asked me to name the single greatest attribute I look for in leaders. "Vulnerability," I responded. My reply surprised him; he expected something else. But I see vulnerability as the key to success in life.

Vulnerability helps me to realize that *every day* I have something new to learn and to connect. I don't know everything, and it's okay for me to acknowledge the fact. Many leaders see vulnerability as a form of weakness, and since they feel very afraid to show any weakness, they avoid vulnerability. To the contrary, I consider vulnerability a sign of great strength. As I become vulnerable, I give permission to others to be vulnerable. And as we are vulnerable together, we become much stronger as a whole.

Through vulnerability, we are prepared to get out in front with our point of view—knowing we might get shot at—while simultaneously encouraging those around us to state their own opinions. Vulnerability allows us to create more influence and better relationships, and paradoxically also gives us a greater sense of self-confidence. It allows us to hold ourselves accountable and also enables us to give significant grace to others.

- *Makes possible long-term gain.*

    The process of integration may create short term difficulties (it takes time, after all), but inevitably it gives us long term gain. Integration helps us to keep mindful of the balance between doing what we need to do *now* and what we need to do over the long term. I don't need to tell you that the pressure is continually on for performance now: "What have you done for me lately?" The process of integration helps us to focus our eyes on the end result and not cave in to counterproductive, short-term pressures.

It Takes Extended Thinking

Integration takes extended thinking time. The best solution doesn't often just magically appear.

We were able to integrate our disparate businesses at Coldwell Banker because I thought through the situation. I studied it. I did all kinds of research. You look hard for ways to do things better. You ask yourself, "Is it possible to take this thing and that thing, even though they seem disconnected, and integrate them in a way that gives us a bigger bang for our buck?" That takes time.

I always start with questions. If I were working with the church mentioned earlier, for example, I might say, "Help me to understand. Why do you do this over here?" After they explained it, I might ask, "And why you do host this event over here?" After they explained that piece, I might ask, "Have you ever thought about how you might integrate the two things to get a bigger return for a smaller investment?"

Integration requires extended time in your head. It doesn't mean taking action quite yet. It's vigorously exercising your brain cells, looking for a better way to do things, probably something out of the norm.

I've worked with many leaders who didn't want to take the time to step back and think. They resisted taking a step back to understand their business as a whole, to understand why they did what they were doing. They didn't want to think through the question, "What is my strategic intent? What do I ultimately want to accomplish?" They thought it would take too much time.

With leaders like these, I often ask, "How serious are you, really, about making a difference? Or do you just want to live in the world you're already in?" I don't hide the fact that those who want to live differently may have to do some things they really don't want to do, things that may not even seem "right" at first. But I tell these leaders, "I promise you that if you do this, and if you do it consistently for a period of time, you will begin to see the kind of results that you really want."

My experience tells me that even busy people who don't think they have the time for this, usually do have the time. I may ask to see the person's schedule and then say, "Tell me about this item on your schedule. What's its purpose?" Almost always, much of what the person is doing doesn't really need to be done, at least by him or her.

Some will insist, "No, really, I just have no white space. I can't do it."

"Okay," I may say. "Although I know this will work for you, if you can't do these basic beginning points, then when you finally decide something has to change, call me and we'll see if I can help. But even before then, I'd like you to think about calling a few people to see what's happened in their lives. Because this does make a difference."

But again, the difference it makes doesn't necessarily occur all at once. I once consulted with a business over several years. Its leaders tended to act autocratically and were very hard on their employees. And yet they frequently told me, "We want to help build families and honor God while we do it." Their hearts were in the right place, but they didn't see how they acted in ways opposite to their intentions. It took a long time and a lot of effort to integrate their conception of themselves with the reality of their actions. When you're dealing with decades of entrenched behavior, the integration piece can take a long time.

Integration may also take a long time when you have to deal with damaged or skewed psyches. Leaders need to learn how to encourage their people and help them to address their discouragement. I've done this by saying, "Let's just take a break. And let's remember where we started from, okay? You have this ideal goal out here, and you feel as though you're moving backwards instead of forwards. But you haven't really moved backwards. In the aggregate, you've really moved forward. You're making some very good things happen. I'm encouraged for you."

As a leader, have you ever received that kind of encouragement? How often do you hear someone telling you, "Look, some good things are happening in this area. Things are changing for the better"? Everyone needs encouragement. While I've always been willing to bust someone who needs busting, I also know that everyone needs appropriate, authentic encouragement. You do. And so do your coworkers.

The Importance of Tone

Tone is important when we speak with others in our attempt to integrate what we know. Some types of questioning can feel very off-putting. We can ask our questions in a way that makes the person feel like a blooming idiot, or we can ask those questions in a truly inquisitive way: "That's really interesting. It looks like you're doing both this and that. I wonder, could there be a way to do these things together in a manner that might work better? Help me to understand." All of a sudden, we're *in* the problem *with* the person, trying to find a satisfying resolution together, rather than saying, "Why haven't you figured this out, you moron?"

The "help me to understand" approach frequently elicits responses like, "You know, I hadn't thought about that. Maybe . . . ."

I've found that the soft approach, in nearly every case, works better than the hard approach.

Tonality includes not merely the sound of our voice, but also includes our body language. What messages are we sending, in addition to the words we say? It's vital to watch our own personal "tonality." Are we being authentic, or are we merely putting on a show?

More often than not in my leadership, I've tried to utilize the Oreo affect: Affirm–Challenge–Affirm. First, affirm the individual; then, honestly broach the topic of the challenge; and finally, find another reason to affirm the person, before ending the conversation. In this way, I hope to bring the relationship back full circle.

Many years ago, a senior executive at one of our companies made a very poor decision, one that he never should have made. The situation required a confrontation. Yet I knew this employee had done a great deal worthy of applause.

When I called him in to my office, I first reminded him of his strengths and the good decisions he'd made to help the organization. I then transitioned to his poor decision. I told him it was unacceptable and would not be tolerated in the future. I called it a serious misjudgment. In fact, he had not taken the time to integrate all of the information available to him to make the best decision possible. As you might imagine, he felt devastated.

But I took care to conclude our time together by reminding him of some other very good decisions he had made in the past, and how confident I felt that he would make similar decisions in the future. That's the Oreo Effect: Affirm—Confront—Affirm. It helps leaders to convey a positive tone that invites colleagues to do better. And isn't that the point?

A Whole Life Enterprise

Most business leaders I've met focus almost exclusively on what they do in their professional lives. But for me, integration is a holistic, whole life enterprise. Two very personal stories illustrate the principle.

Shortly after college, I had to have knee surgery. At the time, I was single and in transition from one city and job to another. I had assumed I would have to find a way to take care of myself. But a relatively new friend at work invited me to recuperate at his home following my surgery. While I like to think of myself as a giver, I find it difficult to be a receiver. In this case, this man and his wife took me in and helped me through the early days after my operation. He illustrated for me the possibility of integrating the personal (someone who needed a place to recover) with the professional (helping a promising young employee).

Some years later, after enjoying some significant career success, two other executives and I decided to start our own firm. One of my neighbors, a university professor, did not fully understand how such a venture might work out. He saw me simply as a neighbor without a job, and he felt concerned for my family. "Greg," he told me, "if you lose your house because you can't pay the mortgage, you can move in with us." His expression of care—offering to intentionally integrate his personal life with my professional life—profoundly affected me and influenced me in both my career and in my personal relationships. I am forever grateful for the invaluable lesson my former neighbor taught me.

Somewhere in all of us there's a core, a core of what we believe regarding what we want to achieve in life. That core affects every aspect of our existence, whether professionally or personally. How do I integrate all of the different aspects of my being in such a way that my core remains intact? This is not an easy objective to achieve. It takes a lot of work, a lot of insight and a lot of self-awareness.

Just this morning, I spoke with a young executive about his own sense of core. How did he integrate his objectives, I wondered, whether in regard to his professional goals or his personal ones? On some days, he admitted, he sees this integration as a major struggle. Today, I encouraged him to continue to find ways to integrate his goals and objectives for his professional growth with his goals and objectives for his personal growth. Regarding the latter, he's told me more than once that he wants to build a strong marriage. I thought it important this morning to remind him that protecting his core is not a chore, but is rather a fundamental key to helping him become all that he wants to be.

Most leaders I've met are looking for a better family life. But when they feel stressed in their jobs, they bring that stress home with them. How do they deal with it? I talk very openly about this, because when I was leading corporations, I wasn't as cognizant of these things as I should have been. Back then, when somebody said to me, "Can you come to do this?" more often than not, I'd say, "Sure," and then fly away somewhere to do it.

While I like to think that I was there for the important things in my kids' lives, I wonder today if maybe it's more vital to be there for the not-so-important things. And not just for my kids. My own first marriage failed, at least in part because I didn't put into it the kind of energy that I now wish I had. Sure, I did really well at my job. I did well with my leadership of non-profit organizations. But I have no problem saying to leaders, "Do you really want to be like me in your personal life?" All of a sudden, the dynamics start to shift.

As leaders, are we truly interested in the whole person, or are we looking just to get what we can from an individual, without understanding how we can give back? This sense of giving of ourselves to others is at the heart of fully integrating our understanding of others.

At one former company where I worked, our leadership team began to understand integration as a means to investigate how we could best develop and support the whole person. We didn't want to think of our employees merely as work units who performed a needed function. We wanted to see how we might help them to integrate all aspects of their life in such a way that they would perform their work in extraordinary ways, but also enjoy extraordinary personal lives in their own regard.

I think of life as a set of columns, with a personal column, a family column, a friend column and a professional column. The question becomes, am I fully aware of each of these columns and the needs I have in connection with each of them? While it's no easy task to address each column, in my experience, those who begin to understand and function appropriately in each of the columns by integrating them to a high degree, tend to have the most rewarding lives.

Not long ago I was asked to sit in on the corporate strategic planning meetings of an organization, first as an observer and later as a facilitator. One day, in the middle of the meeting, the leader got a call: His father was dying. He made it clear to us that he didn't intend to leave the meeting. Two or three of us said to him, "Hey, this is your father. It's more important than what we're doing here. Go to your Dad." And he left. Immediately, the whole dynamic of the meeting shifted for the better. Life works best when a win for one column never means a serious loss for another.

Scooting Down the Road

Many years ago, I decided to buy a small Honda scooter, just for fun. One day as I drove the scooter down the road, wearing my full-face helmet, an acquaintance and his two young boys drove by. The boys pointed at the old coot riding his motor scooter and began to laugh. "What a funny old man!" they said.

The father told me later he used the incident as an integrative moment for his children. "What do you know about the driver?" he asked them. "What kind of work does he do? Where does he live?" Of course, the boys didn't know. They didn't know the funny old man with the big helmet was an acquaintance of Dad's who ran a large, international organization.

The father wanted to help his sons avoid reaching false conclusions based on erroneous assumptions. He wanted them instead to learn how to take the data they could see—an old man riding a motor scooter—and then ask appropriate questions to learn more, finally integrating all the information to better understand the real story.

That's integration, and it works the same way in business as it does in life. So if it works with funny old men with heads shrouded in full-face helmets cruising along on their little scooters, then rest assured it'll work both in your business and in your life.

Implementation

Taking Action, the Most Difficult Step

Many years ago I owned a regional NASCAR racing team. My son was our driver. Over the years, he became very good and won a number of races, as well as series championships.

One day, our crew chief made an astute observation that, at first, I didn't understand, especially in the context of racing. "You must go slow to go fast," he insisted.

What did *that* mean? His comment seemed to make no sense. How could you possibly go *faster* by going *slower*? But eventually it dawned on me: Racetracks always have corners. And several factors determine how fast you can enter and leave those corners—the tightness of the corner, the steepness of the bank, the width of the track. On some tracks, you can enter fast and exit fast. On other tracks, if you enter the corner too fast, it will take you too long to recover and you will throw yourself out of race contention. So he was really saying, "Know the track, know the corner, and know how fast you can go into the corner. When you modify your driving to reflect those realities, you'll be able to leave the corner at your top rate of speed and thus have the best shot at winning the race."

So for NASCAR, here's the principle: Know the track on which you're running, and then based on that information, take appropriate action so that you can compete for the checkered flag. That may mean you have to go slow (in places) to go fast (and win).

The principle is remarkably similar for winning in business and in life. Get to know the nature of the challenges ahead of you, and then based on that information, take appropriate action so that you can come out on top. In Five I's language, that means immerse yourself in the first three I's, then put the pedal to the metal with the fourth I, implementation. Get out there and go. You might have to go slow to go fast, but the goal is to win.

What Is Implementation?

While the first three I's are primarily intellectual activities, implementation is an action step that requires us to actually *do* something with the information we've gathered and processed. Implementation is the only one of the five I's that demands some outwardly visible course of action. Once we've learned, we've integrated, and we've made the best choices we can, now it's time to act.

One young executive with whom I enjoy spending time says, "Implementation is where we apply our mental models, through our personal power, to choose our actions." Effective implementation must come from the basis of our work in the prior three I's. This allows for appropriate decision making, in a timely way, fully integrated with our core objectives.

Implementation is the only step that changes anything outside of our own head. While implementation without the other I's limits us to our existing mental models (which always will be incomplete), focusing on the other I's without implementation makes us, at best, into academic analysts of others' experiences.

More than two decades ago, I chaired the Board of Visitors for Wheaton College. I soon discovered that new faculty, after their second or third year at Wheaton, had to write a paper showing how in their discipline they integrated faith and learning. The papers went in the author's personnel file, and that was it.

I surprised some people when I asked to start reading the papers; nobody had ever made such a request. I quickly found that many of these faculty members wrote some wonderful essays, several of them intellectually potent enough to warrant a book. Over the years, I probably read fifty of those papers. But I would say that maybe two or three of them, and at most four, made any effort to explain how their insights had any application outside of the classroom. The vast majority of the papers did an eloquent job of explaining how the authors integrated faith and learning in their disciplines, but less than a handful explained how one might integrate faith and learning with *living*.

The Wheaton papers remind me that while intellectual exercises are good, if we never work at a practical outpouring of those ideas, they just stay in the head and change nothing outside the skull. If we *really* want to affect anything around us, then such insights have to make their way out of our brains and into some kind of practical action that makes a difference in the world.

Won't It Just Go Away?

My experience over many years tells me that, for many people, implementation is the most difficult of the five I's. Sometimes, the person does not do enough observation and integration and so makes decisions based on too little information. At other times, the individual never quite gets past the idea of thinking to acting. And at still other times, a leader nurtures the false hope that some troublesome problem will just go away on its own.

I sometimes get asked to attend a board meeting for this or that company, as an observer. After one such board meeting, I was asked to interview a few senior staff, including some individuals I hadn't yet gotten to know. And then we came back together with the principals. When I returned from the interviews,, the owners said, "What do you think?"

"I'll start off, but I'm not going where you think I'm going," I said. "This isn't the first time I've been here. I talk to you guys periodically. And what I've been hearing, not directly, is that Bill needs to go."

"Aahh," they replied. "But he's been here for almost two decades."

"This isn't the first time we've talked about it," I said. "I know he's a really good guy."

"Yeah," they agreed, "he's a really good guy."

"*Everybody* says he's a really good guy," I agreed, "but I can't find anybody who wants to report to him. He's still doing the stuff you used to do when you were very small company, and now you're a multi-million dollar company on your way to even bigger things. The people you're hiring are better than he is. Bill is trying to lead them, but he just can't. It isn't working."

"Well, what are we going to do?" they replied. "Maybe the problem will just go away." And then they added, "Or we can just allocate Bill's work to other places."

"Yes, you could do that," I said, "but by doing that, you're going to hurt your company. You're going to slow down. Do you realize that you may put your whole company at risk over this one decision? If you can't keep good people, then you won't be able to do the business you're already doing, and on top of that, you'll stop growing the way you have been growing—and all because of one guy. So, what are you going to do?"

They hemmed and hawed, but they refused to commit to any definite course of action. "We'll see," they finally said.

"I'm not saying that you don't treat him extraordinarily well," I continued. "Bill's been here a long time. You can afford it. You're making good money. But he needs to go."

I know a personnel decision like this is hard. The man wasn't doing anything wrong, either morally or ethically. He simply could no longer do what the company needed him to do. He lacked the right capacity, the appropriate skills and training. He was a penlight battery asked to light up a whole office building.

Great guy, wrong slot.

I interact with a lot of organizations that find themselves in a very similar boat. Maybe the leader has remained in the top position for a long time, but what he's done for decades no longer works. Since he's been there forever, however, nobody is willing to say, "Hey, maybe it's time you found a new challenge." And even though everybody knows where the problem lies, they're unwilling to say it out loud or to do anything about it . . . until the enterprise starts going under. And at that point, it's multiples of times harder to get things realigned.

I try to help leaders understand that as the head of an organization, their first and foremost responsibility is to the organization. If that means some people have to go, then they have to go. At the same time, while those people are there, even if the leader has to help them exit, they get treated extraordinarily well. On the other hand, as an employee, my first and foremost responsibility is to myself. But while I work for the organization, I give everything I have to help it succeed.

That's exactly what I tried to say last week in regard to the wonderful man who needed to go. As the leader, you can never lose sight of the big picture, which is, your company comes first. But you need to treat your people right, too. So what would it mean to treat this man right? It's not keeping him in a job where he has no chance of success. He's become an anchor on the company, and almost certainly, he's not feeling great about himself, either. He knows he's out of his depth, but he's been there so long, he won't quit on his own.

I suspect Bill goes home frustrated most nights, because he knows he's not doing the job. He's *got* to know. He's not stupid; he's smart. And he recognizes the frustration overflowing from both sides. He sits in meetings where he should be contributing, but he doesn't because he can't. He knows it. We know it. The leaders are the only ones who can pull the trigger on what must be done, but to this point, they have refused.

Will the situation just go away on its own? Not unless someone dies . . . or the company does.

Implementation really is the hardest of the five I's. But it's absolutely indispensable.

Overcoming Fear

Fear is often the major stumbling block that prevents leaders from pulling the trigger. So how can leaders overcome those fears and take appropriate action? One place to begin is to understand that each decision and action is just one step along a longer process. The biggest crises tend to result not from implementing some uncertain action step, but from refusing to implement anything at all.

Implementation can have something of a stair-step nature. A first step may be quite small, but as your muscles and experience grow, you can start taking larger steps. Fear often starts dissipating when you understand that, in most cases, you don't have to do everything all at once. If you see that you need to make a move, you can begin the process by taking a single step. And as you gain experience and confidence in implementing, based on what you've learned, your leg muscles grow stronger, enabling you to take longer and steeper steps.

Or let's change the picture a bit. Have you ever seen a crab moving on the beach? He moves forward sideways. He moves ahead, but not in a straight line. You and I can learn something from the crab.

If you have a target you want to reach that lies forward of your current position, you don't always have to get there along a straight line. Sometimes, you can't get there by moving in a straight line. The key to moving forward by going sideways is to *just make some moves*. If you never move off of the starting point—if you never take some kind of action, even if that action is a sideways move—you'll never reach your target.

Think of an archer. After he shoots his arrow, he learns where he hit the target. With that knowledge, he adjusts his aim and shoots again, always intent on hitting the bullseye. He continually adjusts his decisions to accomplish his goal in light of prevailing conditions. For the archer, it's all about taking action and making adjustments. It's the same in leadership.

Of course, movement is of little use unless you have an idea where you want to go. What are your goals? Growing organizations and leaders always set goals for themselves. These goals, whether corporate or personal, must be realistic and achievable, but also should require us to stretch.

Too often I have found extremes in regard to goal setting. I may be a good implementer, but if my goals are unrealistic, I probably won't accomplish much—and goals not regularly accomplished become a major disincentive. On the other hand, if our goals and expectations don't stretch us, then we will never discover our full capacity.

Another way to address fear is to ask yourself, what do you actually control? What can you actually control? Understanding those two things should have a powerful effect on your ability and willingness to take action. If we focus on issues extraneous to the core of whatever we want to accomplish, we can easily get distracted by things outside of our control and consequently fail to move forward on those things that we do (or can) control. Keeping our focus for implementation on the things that we do and can control allows us to move down the path we've chosen. But we still have to act.

In this process of implementing an action step, we grow into excellence. By exercising the muscle of action, we learn and grow, and over time, we make better decisions. As we do so, we learn how to empty ourselves and to give ourselves time to be refilled with new experiences and new learning. As we do, fear becomes less and less of an obstacle to our decision making.

A senior executive once asked me about how to get from one point in his strategic thinking and planning to another. "When you travel from one of your locations to another," I asked, "are you always able to drive in a straight line, as the crow flies?" The answer, of course, was "no." So we discussed the idea that going from point A to point B may require any one of a number of turns or apparent detours along the way. The question is, are we making progress toward our goals with each turn we make? In some cases, it might appear (and could be true) that we're moving backward for period of time before we can start moving forward again. In those cases, sideways movement is not the enemy; stagnation is. Movement is the key.

We can't let our fear control us by keeping us from taking steps, however small, toward our goal. We must make our decisions and then act on them. Beware of spending significant amounts of time wrestling with what won't work and debating alternative solutions, all for the purpose of deferring some action you fear taking! If you understand this aspect of your internal self, then you can begin to accept that every decision and action you take is not the last, nor should it be. Each decision and each action is simply a step along life's journey; but you can't take that journey unless you begin taking some steps. You will never discover what's around the corner unless you take some steps to go around the corner.

When Style Becomes a Hurdle

Sometimes we hesitate to take significant action because we get hung up on style. When I was a young executive, one of my responsibilities was to write a monthly report for some of our large, institutional clients. The CEO of the company always insisted on reviewing the report prior to sending it to the client.

I began to notice that every month, for some reason, he found it necessary to make changes to whatever anyone else had written. It seemed to me as though the editing exercise was more about his style rather than the actual content. In fact, I suspected it was a form of control. He wanted others to know that only *he* had the capacity and the ability to communicate appropriately to the client. But that didn't bother me as much as the fact that his habit slowed down the whole process and created some unnecessary problems.

One month, I took a copy of his edited report from the month before and altered only the date, then submitted that version to him for his review. True to form, he made a number of additional changes to the document, all gratuitous, thus confirming my suspicions.

I subsequently arranged to have a meeting with the CEO to show him the two documents. I tried to help him see the counterproductive nature of his actions. Although it's a small incident that took place many decades ago, I never forgot it. The point for us today is that, as executives and leaders, we can get so concerned about style that we effectively fail to move past the first three I's into productive, goal-reaching implementation. Style has its place, but it becomes a problem when it gets in the way of implementing actions that help us to reach our goals.

Influence Up and Down

Leaders who take effective action can influence their organizations positionally, both up and down. They say to their people, in both words and deeds, "I will do whatever I need to do in order to help you succeed in all of life." Such servant leaders enjoy remarkable influence wherever they go.

If we become people of action, decision makers, implementers, then the people who report to us will consistently look to us for direction. Similarly, the people to whom we report also will begin to look to us for possible next steps. While having such influence can put a lot of pressure on those willing to take the risk of moving ahead and taking steps beyond data-gathering and integration, it's worth it.

When we become strong implementers, we also bring clarity to those we lead. Regardless of the position or job we hold, we all need clarity. In my experience, leaders who by their actions bring clarity to their work objectives spark a significantly higher performance level among their coworkers, along with creating a far more rewarding work environment. Taking consistent action also helps the people who report to you get a strong sense of your personality, which encourages them to do their work with confidence.

Does all this seem like a lot to manage? It helps me, at least, to think of these things in the context of what it means to be a servant leader. A servant leader, as I describe it, is one who serves both up and down the organization. Usually, we think of a servant as someone who serves an individual of higher rank or authority. But it is equally important that leaders learn to serve those they lead. My philosophy of servant leadership directs me to do whatever might be required in order to help my colleagues, whether "up" or "down" from me, succeed in all of life.

Many years ago, a man I consider my greatest mentor taught me both verbally and through his life what it meant to truly be a servant of others. Because he consistently acted on his beliefs and on what he understood to be true—he never shrank from implementation, in other words—his influence worldwide has grown incredibly wide. While he never made it his objective to become hugely influential, one day at a time he has aimed to encourage everyone within his reach. Throughout his life he has doggedly held to that philosophy, and as a result, he has seen an incredible number of leaders he has influenced begin to significantly impact their own worlds.

The Importance of Delegation

Implementing action steps and doing things, rather than just thinking about them, doesn't mean that you have to do everything on your own. Delegation can be an incredibly important part of implementation.

Nevertheless, one of the most difficult tasks of implementation for many senior executives and leaders is the idea of truly becoming delegators. More often than not, the leaders I have known talk about delegating far more than they actually do it. It's difficult for highly capable leaders, who may rightly see themselves as intellectually superior to many of their colleagues, to believe that by delegating some task and releasing control and encouraging others to take action based on their own experiences, that the end result will lead to a more successful company. And so they refuse to delegate . . . and as a result, they often become the chief bottlenecks that keep their companies from growing.

I try to do only those things that I alone can do, and then delegate to others the tasks that they can do better than I can. Effective leaders learn how to delegate to others out of their comfort zones, but still within the realm of their abilities. I want to become a facilitator for those I work with, not a controller. I want to help them become all they possibly can be by encouraging them to take appropriate and necessary action steps.

Dealing with Criticism

Every leader knows that the actions he or she takes in any given set of circumstances can generate an avalanche of criticism. But criticism comes with leadership. It then becomes important for us as leaders to differentiate between criticism that leads toward improvement and emotional criticism that simply tears down.

I once made a personnel decision to remove an executive from his post, sparking criticism not only from the employee but also from a member of the Human Resources department and from those impacted by my action to dismiss their leader. I heard more than once that my actions seemed inconsistent with my earlier promises to act as a servant leader.

As a servant leader, however, I knew that I had to be prepared to stand up to the criticism that inevitably comes from misunderstanding or disagreement. In this case, I believed that, in the long term, I had done what was best for the whole organization. I had to keep in mind not only the organization's needs, but also what we could do to make the transition the least traumatic possible for the employee involved.

To the very best of my ability, I had tried to make a clearly bad situation into the very best one we could still achieve. I didn't find my confrontation with the individual pleasant, nor should I have. Yet at the same time, I tried my best to demonstrate the potential that could come out of a clearly bad set of circumstances. Additionally, I considered it important to hear out those who felt undervalued or taken advantage of by my decision.

All along the way, I had to remain confident that the decision I made really was in the best interests of all concerned. Having that confidence also meant that I needed to very carefully weigh and assess and understand my underlying motivations. Today I'd call this "the necessity of developing internal affective communication." I had to learn to confront myself as well as those with whom I worked. Did my action move us toward our ultimate goal? Was I okay with movement rather than stagnation, so long as that movement helped us reach our ultimate objective? After I acted, I took the time to reassess. With what I had learned, I sought to be refilled. I learned to be an apologist for what we were doing, not a controller.

As leaders, we can seem very confident, even when we're not. Frankly, many times we're pretty good actors (and often have to be). But I wanted to balance my actions and my confidence, or purported confidence, with a check of understanding my baseline motivation. Did I truly want to secure the best situation for the organization, even while remaining appropriately concerned for the individual? I had no choice but to wrestle with those issues. I think good leadership demands nothing less.

Most of all, however, I had to be willing to act. I couldn't allow criticism to keep me from pulling a trigger that I knew had to get pulled.

Pull the Trigger

Many leaders love to go through the process of the first three I's. They love it because so long as they're thinking, reflecting and data gathering, they never have to make a decision.

Think of the archer again. He's aiming at a large, circular target adorned with a series of concentric circles, a bullseye in the center. Imagine the archer getting ready to shoot. He picks an arrow. He fits it to the string. He aims. He adjusts his line of sight. But until he shoots, is he really an archer? At some point, he needs to let the arrow fly. If he doesn't let the arrow fly, he will never know if his preparation ever led to anything.

I recently spent time with a senior executive who, over the course of several months, had discussed with me a number of decisions he needed to make. At the end of our recent time together, he said, "I guess I need to pull the trigger." He clearly didn't want to. Similar to the hesitant archer, this executive continued to focus on the "ready" and "aim" part of the equation, but felt unsure whether his "ready" and "aim" even faced in the right direction.

Contrast that example with that of another executive I worked with extensively. He had the opportunity to buy the business he'd operated for a long time. I helped him work through his options regarding the best way to purchase the company. For example, he could buy the company, inclusive of all assets and liabilities; but many times, this is not the best way to acquire a business, since you take on both known and unknown liabilities. Second, he had to consider the timing of the purchase. In this particular case, the company's cash flow varied significantly throughout the year.

After some discussion and a lot of thought, he pulled the trigger on a proposal, contingent on a high cash flow period which would require him to raise far less capital. The owners accepted his proposal, he acquired the company, and over several years, he managed to grow and expand the business and eventually sell it at a substantial profit.

Because he had done his homework—he'd carefully worked through the first three I's—he felt confident enough to implement his decision to buy the company. He understood the risks involved in his undertaking and he pulled the trigger just as soon as it made best sense to do so. He's never looked back.

Take the Risk

Simply pulling the trigger doesn't guarantee that everything we choose to do will come out as we want it to or expect it to. Every time we pull the trigger, we take a risk. That's just the nature of life, and of leadership. We just need to keep in mind that by refusing to pull the trigger—if our time with the first three I's tells us that pulling the trigger makes sense—we usually take a much bigger risk.

Many years ago at a large organization, our leadership team made a decision to try a totally new approach to the business. The new strategy would borrow many aspects from our old structure, but in other areas it would totally revamp the familiar approach. We recruited a senior executive within the organization to relocate to a major city to try out the new idea. It was certainly a risk for him, and neither he nor the organization had a clue of whether it would succeed. We had done our research, we made our decision, and we acted by hiring an outstanding executive. We also provided more than adequate capital.

The experiment failed.

The good news is that we had tried something. We didn't just analyze the data. We'd put all the best possible pieces of the puzzle together, and yet in the end we discovered the idea did not work. The initiative didn't fail for lack of capital or scarcity of good leadership; we learned the idea simply would not work in the real world, at least at that time.

Did the failure discourage us? To some extent, of course it did. But more importantly, we demonstrated to the entire organization, at a critical time, that we were prepared to make decisions, take risks, take steps to understand what had happened, and then make another decision. We would not stand still.

Implementation is really about action versus reaction. Are we prepared to be innovators? Are we prepared to go out on a limb, unabashedly? Or are we like those who react rather than act? Reactionaries can tell us all about what would have been better; yet they themselves wouldn't dare be the first ones to take a step forward.

By choosing to become persons of action, I realize that we may have to give up something in the short term for the possibility of greater opportunity or better results in the long term. But I also know that action-oriented people have a far better chance of gaining long-term opportunities than do the reactionaries.

Still, never imagine that it's about becoming a "doing" person rather than a "thinking" person. In fact, it's about both. It's about becoming a thinking/doing person. The best leaders are those who strike the proper balance between the first three I's and this fourth one, implementation. The question is, can you be that kind of person? I have no doubt that you can. I encourage you to continually ask yourself, "How much more can I profitably learn, and how much do I lose by not acting on what I've learned?"

It's true that not everything we choose to do will yield the expected results. Take the risk anyway.

The Beauty of Implementation

Poseurs often talk about what might've been or what they would have done. But they never did it. That is the beauty of implementation: We actually do something.

Do we always do it right? No. Do we make mistakes? Of course. But when we implement, we are in the battle and not just talking about it.

The owners of Coldwell Banker Corporation recruited me many years ago because at that time, the company needed and wanted to change. "We want you at Coldwell Banker because we need you to help change the culture here," they told me.

"But I don't know about residential real estate," I objected. "In my lifetime, I've bought and sold two houses. That's all I know about it. I know nothing more."

"Maybe," they replied, "but you know how to run companies and you know how to affect culture. You can learn about the industry by hiring people with residential real estate expertise." I accepted their offer, but frankly, my coming caused a lot of consternation for those who had been used to the way Coldwell Banker had always done things.

The creation of Coldwell Banker University was my attempt to shake up the company's whole way of doing its organizational development training. The company itself was a huge, fifty thousand person national organization doing hundreds of thousands of transactions a year. When I arrived, it had in place all the traditional training strategies. As I started looking at the system through a newbie's eyes, it troubled me that everything seemed so theoretical. It didn't seem practical on the organizational development level. And on the training side, it offered only very basic kinds of help: How do you get a listing? How do you fill out paperwork? It focused almost entirely on our agent base, with essentially nothing for corporate staff or other associates.

As I began to ponder the situation, I started hearing from our managers and leaders about growing numbers of disaffected and discontented people. "Well, if somebody's discontented," I told myself, "they're not going to be very productive. And that means they're going to talk to their coworkers, which will keep them from being productive. So maybe there are some practical reasons we should rethink this."

I then started thinking once more about servant leadership. And I asked myself, "Don't we, as a company, also have a responsibility to the people who work for us? Shouldn't we provide them with holistic resources, so that they can build better lives for themselves?"

So we redid our whole approach, created Coldwell Banker University, and hired about seventy faculty members, all of them Masters-level experts and above from around the country. We began to develop a whole curriculum of courses that anyone in the organization could pick from, regardless of their position.

Some people in the organization shook their heads, because they didn't see how the new approach had anything to do with our business. And from a historical point of view, it didn't. But from my point of view, it had everything to do with our business and also with our obligation as a company.

And without question, it made a difference. I still hear from people today who like to tell me what they gained from Coldwell Banker University.

But you lead because you believe. And at the end of the day, we had a very good bottom line, so clearly the initiative didn't kill us. I can't prove it, but I still think CBU helped us to turn the ship around. It wasn't the only thing, but it helped.

And from my perspective, that's the beauty of implementation.

Implication

Assessing All of Our Life Experiences

Before most publishers decide to contract a manuscript, they go through an exercise to estimate how many of the proposed books they would have to sell in the first year of publication to make the book a financial success. If they believe they can sell at least that number, then usually the author of the manuscript gets a contract to publish the book.

A friend who has worked for many years in the publishing industry tells me that he once worked for a publisher that always went through this process, but so far as he knows, it never again revisited those numbers after the book's release. The company didn't return to those sales estimates after the book had been out for a year to see whether, in fact, the book had sold as many copies as the publisher thought it needed to sell. The initial sales estimates just went in a file somewhere and stayed there forever.

Because the company never evaluated whether its sales forecasts indeed resembled its actual sales numbers, it never made any adjustments to how it generated the forecasts. That meant it never improved its ability to make the critical forecasts.

You can probably guess what eventually happened.

Although the company published a lot of good books and won a slew of literary awards, after a few years it had to be sold. Because it didn't evaluate whether it had accomplished what it intended to accomplish—and just as importantly, understand why its forecasts either hit the mark or didn't— it laid the groundwork for its eventual forced sale.

The fifth I, *implication,* is all about assessing what we have done and evaluating our results to see whether what we expected to happen actually happened, and to understand why it did or did not work. Like all of the I's, implication is indispensable.

A college classmate of mine, for example, took a job after college as an elementary schoolteacher at a boarding school for missionary children in Kenya, East Africa. On one of her early visits back to the States, she admitted to a group of us that she had been struggling with her choice of career, wondering whether she was accomplishing as much as some of her co-workers. But her outlook changed, she said, once she recognized that she felt called to be the very best elementary education school teacher *she* could possibly be. After wrestling with the implications of her job choice, she decided on her next step of implementation. Her keen ability to make that assessment, followed by her making an appropriate decision that took her on a subsequent course of action, had a remarkable influence on my own life. Her story reminds me, to this day, that the process of implication empowers us to become better in every aspect of life.

What Is Implication?

If implementation is the hardest thing for most of us, then implication is the most important. Many of us, after making some decision and moving forward, sort of wipe the ground and say, "Whew, I made that decision! Now I don't need to worry about it anymore." And so we neglect to take time to reflect on whether what we expected to happen actually happened.

We therefore don't ask ourselves, "What took place as a result of making that decision? Did we achieve what we wanted to achieve? If not, why not? What are our current choices, now that we understand what's happened? Do we need to just let it go on as it is? Do we need to drop it altogether? Do we need to make modifications one way or another? And do we have the right people in place to continue the progress we've enjoyed so far?"

Implication means asking the question, "What do we know and what don't we know?" It requires admitting a level of uncertainty, because knowing and assuming are not close to being the same thing. We may assume that we know why we got a particular result, but until we actually investigate and make enough inquiries to really find out, we don't know. Implication drives us to know rather than to feel content with merely assuming.

After we implement some action step, therefore, we absolutely must understand the results. Did we expect them? What unexpected consequences may have taken place? What could we do better if we were to decide again on a similar course of action?

Implication is a special case of being inquisitive about the real world experiments to which we subject our mental models. It's closing the learning loop so we can iterate *ad infinitum*. Implication helps us to reflect on how to implement differently, if necessary. In the implication stage, we look back to learn, which allows us to focus forward to grow.

Implication reminds us that ideas, in and of themselves, are not the solution. Implication helps us to sift those ideas and evaluate their effectiveness so that we can choose the best ones and either discard or modify the others. As we move through the process of implication, we begin to understand how we can make the kind of changes that lead to better results. Implication, when done right, causes us to stretch and allows us to feel that we're making strides toward some enhanced achievement.

In the implication stage, we return to the very front of the process and start asking questions all over again. We indulge our curiosity. We're intentional. We try to integrate all these pieces and ask ourselves, "Now, what did we learn?" When we do this, we can honestly say, "We're on a continuum of growth as we constantly reflect on the implications of what we've done."

Really, it only makes sense. If we put a lot of work and effort into trying to achieve something, then why would we not want to know if what we had planned and worked hard at and then implemented, really accomplished what we expected it to accomplish? And why wouldn't we want to know what we might learn from the total experience, whether it turned out as we'd hoped or not? *That's* implication.

More than a Hope

Although numbers are a key part of the implication process, it also has a content piece. If you write a book, for example, you probably have some specific intentions for what you want your readers to get out of your work. You want them to learn something in particular, to have the concepts in the book affect them in some identifiable way. You have more than a mere "hope" that your book has a nice effect. You wrote with the "intent" that your book would bring about particular effects.

From my perspective, the danger of using words like "hope" in the implication process is that by using them, we tend to lose the proactive mindset that is essential in bringing about the effects we want.

I spoke recently to an executive about a problem he was having with one of his employees. The exec had coached his co-worker on some specific things he needed the man to do. "Is he going to do what you've asked him to do?" I asked.

"I hope so," he replied.

Ten minutes later, I asked the exec about another issue. "Well, I think so," he answered.

I interrupted the flow of our conversation and said to him, "I want you to hear what you just said to me. Just ten minutes ago, you told me, 'I hope so.' And now you said, 'I think so.' Do you realize that both words are equivocating terms? The problem with equivocating terms is that they let everyone off the hook."

When we do implication correctly, we acknowledge that we're after more than just a nebulous hope. We expect to see something definite, something specific. That's why I want to hear words like "expect" more than I hear words like "hope." There's a life-altering aspect to what we expect. The words we choose do make a difference.

Front and Back

What we do in the implication stage looks a lot like what researchers do in designing their experiments. At the front end, they do "formative research," which helps them to design the experiment in a way that gives them the best chance of acquiring useful results. And at the back end, once the experiment has finished, they do "summative research," which tells them whether they set up and executed the experiment in a way that gave them the results they expected.

Formative research allows you to properly direct your inquiry so you can find out whatever you need to find out. Summative research looks at the aftermath, to see how well your inquiry actually revealed what you intended it to reveal. Did your experiment, in other words, actually measure whatever you expected it to measure?

Since we've been talking a bit about books in this chapter, I've noted that recently some publishers have begun to do something relatively new for the publishing industry. They're regularly sending out little surveys to consumers, brief questionnaires that ask for opinions on book covers, book titles, or sometimes even the content of a book itself. "How much do you like this?" the surveys will ask, "What don't you like about it? What would you like better?"

That's formative research, a part of what I call inquisitiveness. It helps you to make the best decision possible before you create the product and actually "go public" with it. In the old days, publishers tended just to print a bunch of titles, throw them at the wall and hope that enough of them would "stick." So I'd say the new inquisitiveness is a distinct improvement.

But what about what happens at the end of the cycle? Wouldn't it help to know, at the end of the day, if what we thought was right, was in fact, right? That's summative research, what I call implication. Did what we expect to happen, actually happen? What if something didn't work as we thought it would, because we based our expectations on an incorrect assumption, or on a hidden factor that didn't make sense until we saw it plainly? Unless we engage in that kind of implication, we'll never know. And therefore we might repeat the same errors that cost us big the first time around.

Once we feel convinced about some course of action, once we sense it's the right thing to do, we have to take action. But having made that decision and implemented that action step, then it becomes imperative that we revisit the decision and action step and analyze both from various perspectives. How much did the thing actually cost? How much did it actually make? What effect did making it have on our people—what did it cost *them*? What happened that we didn't expect? Did we build this at the expense of that? Did it affect our reputation? Did it bring in more business? Did it give us fresh ideas for something else?

Focus on Principles

The process of implication helps to keep us focused on the priority of principles. Are the principles we're using to help us make our decisions appropriate for our current circumstances? Have we been overly influenced by the latest person with whom we spent time, or do our guiding principles still direct us? Do we have the maturity to listen carefully to a variety of inputs and then assess all of them through the lens of our core principles, so that we may come to valid conclusions about next steps? If we've suffered some failure, does that failure indicate we've used an invalid principle, or rather that we have inadequately implemented that principle?

A few years ago, a company asked me to meet with its principals to help its executives discuss where the firm was and where it hoped to go. At the end of a full day of reviewing their strategy plans, the CEO asked me if I thought it'd been a good day.

"We won't know if it was a good day for at least ninety days," I replied. He looked at me quizzically. "If nothing changes as a result of our conversation today, and if the company stays intractably on the same route it's been on, then, in fact, probably it was not a good day," I explained. "If, however, you stick with the process we exercised throughout the day, fully understanding the implications of your decisions, then, in fact, I think the argument can be made that it has been a good day."

About three months later, after I still had not heard from the company, I called the CEO. The chagrin in his voice alerted me that things had not gone well. "We've been busy," he said, "and we've not been able to address all the changes for the company that we'd agreed upon." He also admitted that the company had not grown and advanced as he'd hoped it would.

"Then it was not a good day," I declared, referring to our lengthy meeting of ninety days before. The CEO had not implemented the action steps that all of us had endorsed, and he had not followed through on the process of implication that we had all affirmed. In other words, he had ignored the basic principles that we had agreed should direct the company's course. And very predictably, that woeful chagrin showed up in his voice three months later.

Read Your Audience

Leaders who want to get proficient at implication need to learn how to "read" their audience. And that usually begins by trying to understand the personalities of the men and women around them.

Do you pull back on the reins to keep someone from charging over a cliff? Or is the person like a horse that doesn't want to leave the starting block and responds only to the whip? In the long run, I think it's almost always better to work with people who need to get reined in a bit. They irritate me on some days, but the irritation is nothing compared to the frustration I feel caused by those who hesitate even to leave the starting block. These people are perpetually afraid to make mistakes, always fearful of taking action, and therefore find it almost impossible to move forward. They never even get to the stage of implication, because they never implement anything.

So let me ask: Do you know your people? Do you know how to "read" your audience?

I once spent some time with a minister who worried that he might not be connecting with his congregation. I helped him to reflect on the question, "Are your people truly able to hear your messages?" I had visited his congregation a few times and noticed each time that although he had very good content, he read his sermons in their entirety, without once looking up. He had very little, if any, eye contact with his people, and therefore virtually no connection to his congregation.

I encouraged him to try a new style. I wanted him to process the fact that although he put significant effort into creating high content material, the people for whom he meant it did not appear to receive it. He took my advice, and by changing his style—doing less reading and having more eye contact—he began to see his people connecting to him and to his messages.

My advice to him dovetailed with the general premise I suggest for all speakers. Speakers essentially need to do two things simultaneously. On the one hand, they're delivering remarks, and on the other hand, they are interpreting the responses they receive from the audience to their comments. Depending on that interpretation, they must adjust what they have to say and how they say it. This, too, is a version of the implication process.

I love to interact with students. A university graduate program once asked me to speak on these very issues to its students and faculty. When I did so, I observed one person sitting off to the side; he didn't appear to engage with me or my subject and frankly, I felt quite disappointed that I couldn't reach him. Following my remarks, however, this individual approached me and not only articulated the key elements of my talk, but added some new thoughts of his own. Despite my conclusion, he had heard, he had engaged, and he had understood. I had totally misinterpreted his actions.

I learned that day that although I had actively tried to divine the response of my audience, I had failed to do so with at least one member of that audience. In the process of implication, I found I had to adjust. I had to recognize that what I believe to be true may not always be true. Yes, we need to learn how to "read" our audiences; but we also need to remember that, sometimes, we misinterpret what we think we read.

One thing that makes it so difficult to do an accurate reading is that we humans possess a wild assortment of emotions that frequently seem to say one thing while actually expressing something quite different. At times, we can't even accurately describe how we ourselves feel; so should it surprise us that sometimes we misread the emotions of others? Even if we can't always accurately read what we think we have, however, it remains important to remember the critical role of human emotions and their power to shape our environment.

We leaders have to remember that emotions have the power to overcome rational decision-making. But if I, as the leader, understand the emotions of those with whom I'm working; if I've tried to recognize what tends to drive them and if I know when they feel most able to move forward (or by contrast, when they tend to feel helpless and uncomfortably constrained); then I'm in a far better position to create the environment that will support that person and help us all move toward the objectives we have in common.

Take Your Time

If we move too quickly through the implication process, we may tend to rush toward unwise changes or feel tempted to make inappropriate adjustments to people or programs. But in the vast majority of cases, we do not have to act as though we're caught in a drag race at the Indianapolis Speedway.

In this regard, I've discovered that the 24-hour rule works very well.

This rule states that very few things need our immediate response. In almost every case, taking the time to reflect about the proposed action, carefully thinking through its implications, leads us to better decisions for the next action step.

In this interim time, I need to understand the difference between a sense of urgency and allowing panic to control my decision-making. Too often, perhaps, we lose clarity on the difference between these two very dissimilar approaches. We also need to keep in mind that something that appears urgent to one person may be perceived as panic by another.

So the next time you find yourself pondering the necessity of making some significant change, I urge you to take 24 hours to mull over your situation. Don't feel the need to act, or even respond, without doing some serious reflection. Remind yourself, "Urgency is not the same thing as panic."

A Period for Affirmation

The implication stage can provide a great period for affirmation, a time for telling your people what they've done well. In the implication phase, we must try to understand the various roles our people have played in achieving whatever we've accomplished as a team. Leadership guru Ken Blanchard insists that this is a wonderful time to tell people what they've done well. It is a time for affirmation, a time when we acknowledge that *all* of us need to feel needed.

A very successful leader who travels the world and who has

been a wonderful friend to me remarked at one of our many lunches that no one had ever told him what I had told him that day. I had simply said, "You're a good man." In truth, that simple affirmation was a good experience not only for him, but a reminder to me of how important it is to recognize the goodness of others who impact our lives in so many ways.

A wonderful and even essential part of affirmation is the knowledge that somebody has our back—and that we are prepared to cover someone else's back. We all need at least one other person whom we trust so implicitly that, regardless of the size of the challenges that confront us, we know that this person loves us more.

I have a very dear friend who's been a mentor to me for a long time. He has now begun a battle with Alzheimer's. He regularly calls me and says, "Greg, we will be friends for life, right?" Of course, I always answer, "yes." I know he has my back and that, no matter what, he'll be there for me, even as many times as he's challenged me on my decisions. Equally so, I cannot imagine any circumstance under which I would not have my friend's back. As leaders, we cannot abandon those whom we have chosen to support and with whom we enjoy a close relationship.

Not long ago, I witnessed a graphic demonstration of what such a commitment means. Few others probably noticed; but I'll never forget it.

The San Clemente Presbyterian Church celebrates communion every Sunday. One weekend, out of the corner of my eye, I saw an older couple come in late. The lady sat in a wheelchair while the man looked very old and feeble. Two caregivers accompanied them, one sitting next to them and the other sitting behind them. I noticed the couple, and then turned my attention elsewhere.

When communion began at the end of the service, I observed two communion servers from the church silently begin to serve communion to this elderly couple. One of the caregivers immediately reached around from behind the lady in the wheelchair, cupping her hand under the woman's chin to prevent any dribbles. Nobody had to say anything; it just happened. No big scene, but a sweet sense of one person genuinely caring for another.

I couldn't help but reflect on what I'd seen. I'd learned something about how this church cares for people, unobtrusively and habitually. Nobody said to the caregivers, "Go serve these elderly people." Instead, I observed people who cared so much about these dear individuals that they paid attention to every detail.

All of us need to feel needed and cared for. We all need affirmation. And while I suppose that nearly any time would be a good time for affirming others, I know that the process of implication provides an especially appropriate time to let others know how much you appreciate them and the contributions they make.

Expect and Manage Conflict

The flip side to affirmation is conflict. Ironically, perhaps, conflict has a tendency to erupt at the implication stage. As we do our implication review, at times conflict arises between different players.

"Well, you may be right that this thing went wrong, but it wasn't my fault. Fred had responsibility for that job on that day."

"What? What are you talking about? I wasn't even there! How can you say I was responsible?"

"It's true you weren't there, but you were supposed to be. Nobody knew where you were."

"How can you say that? I was with Bob the whole day! He made the arrangements a week before. I have the memo to prove it. Do I need to show it to you?"

And on it goes.

I've found that immediate resolution is not always the best course of action. Sometimes, it pays to let the conflict play out, although I admit that such a strategy tends to run counter to my first inclination. I naturally want to try to bring immediate resolution to conflict.

My experience, however, tells me that much value can come from letting conflict play out. For one thing, it allows everyone to know that they're being heard. How I as the leader manage conflict is critical to building a better and more successful organization. And such a strategy still allows me to hold people accountable for what I hired them to do. I have clarity of expectation even as we continually reflect on what we're doing and what we can do better.

The Lowest Common Denominator Effect

As we work at the process of implication, especially when we do so in teams, we have to remain as broad minded and least constricted intellectually as possible. Certainly, we do not want someone with the least experience or capacity in a particular situation to control the organization and everyone in it.

It is therefore important, as we wrestle through the implication of our actions, to carefully avoid what I call the Lowest Common Denominator Effect. This occurs when someone with the least ability to think out-of-the-box controls everyone else in the organization by shooting down any idea that seems risky to him or her.

This "control" usually isn't overt, but covert. Often it isn't intentional. More often than not, the Lowest Common Denominator person is the nicest individual in the group. He or she is the one man or woman in the room least likely to cause conflict—but is equally likely to be the individual least prepared to take a risk. These individuals do not see that their LCD tendency often nudges the organization to move backward, rather than forward or even laterally.

No doubt you've seen it happen, as I have: The person who yells the loudest or insists the most often wins—not because he or she is right, but because the other people at the table get tired of fighting. Rarely is that the way to move forward.

Four Cautions

Implication is hard enough when we have everything going for us. It becomes much more difficult when we remain unaware of four common obstructions to effective implication.

1. *Beware of over-analysis.*

   Some people never think they have quite enough information; they always want to learn more, do more analysis, commission more research. In one context, that thirst for information is good, but for the welfare of the organization, we must be able to move from the purely analytical to taking some action. This remains true even as we contemplate the results of our prior action and as we look forward to our next steps.

2. *Beware of over-action.*

   Equally troubling are those eager to move instantly, without a moment's reflection. We have to rein in these individuals and make sure that, as a team, we spend adequate time in reflection so that we can make the best possible decision.

3. *Beware of assuming that success always follows success.*

   Implication helps us to see that success doesn't always follow success; significant failure may intervene. Understanding both helps us to move forward. I have heard many people say that they learn the most through failure, and I while I don't disagree with them, I would insist that if people have only failure, then they haven't learned how to succeed. Striving toward success, however defined, allows us to move forward at a healthy pace. It builds in us confidence as a whole person.

4. *Beware of becoming a controller rather than a synthesizer.*

   Synthesizers tend to have more success than controllers. Synthesizers can take complex and difficult issues and appropriately assess them, coming to understand the implications of some action step in order to recommend new courses of action. They are collaborative by nature and take into account both their own sensitivities and the concerns of others likely to be impacted by the decisions made. If I choose to be a controller, however, I don't appropriately take into account how I negatively impact others by my actions.

Let Go, Hold Tight

Part of understanding implication is the willingness to let go of certain things, because we've experienced something new and we understand we don't need to go backward. This time of letting go is based on learning something new that works better. So to truly experience the good of the new, we have to let go of the old.

At the same time, as we reflect, we may begin to see that if we are to achieve the same kinds of results we've enjoyed already, we really need to continue in the very same direction we had been going. Change for change's sake is almost never appropriate.

I believe that bringing these two different perspectives together demonstrates the point that leadership without change is just management. Through this process of implication, of understanding why things happened the way they did, we give ourselves the ability to change only those things that can move us forward.

Become a Continuous Learner

Our goal along every step of the way is to *become better*. And that desire to become better requires a commitment to become a continuous learner. I'm continually learning how to become better at what I do and so to become a better person.

We need to display a lot of grace here. We may have to acknowledge upfront that while we're not sure where things are going, we have committed ourselves to identifying and evaluating what did actually happen.

Some people say to me, "Greg, when you talk about implication, you're assuming that the plan is not going to work and that you want to make it better."

"No," I reply, "I'm not assuming that at all. But I am assuming reality, which says there are always things I can do to make the plan better."

The fact is, circumstances change over which I have no control. Since external forces are always at work, even when things seem to be going well, how can I just keep on doing whatever I'm doing? If I'm not doing the necessary implication, if I'm not becoming aware of what's going on, eventually reality will force me to take action. And when I'm *forced* to take action, it's never as good as when I proactively take action. Proactive decisions are always better than reactive ones.

Implication is what makes exponential learning possible. As one friend says, "It's the difference between analyzing a computer program and changing that program to see what the change does. The second is invariably more surprising, and surprises open the door to another cycle of learning."

Be True to You

I mentor a lot of individuals, and I've found that some of them want to be me. But in fact, I'm trying to help them become themselves. Trying to be someone else misses the opportunity for us to become all that we have an opportunity to be.

It's critical in this process of implication that we remain true to ourselves and to who we believe we truly are. What capacities do we have to make a difference?

One way to help yourself remain true to you is by creating a regular appointment with yourself to reevaluate your own commitment level to being you and not someone else. It's great to have heroes. It's great to have mentors. It's great to have a coach. But the best thing you can do for yourself and for your people *is to remain you.*

Model It

Implication becomes powerful and gets regularly practiced within an organization only when the leader models it. If I don't respect the implication process, no one else will, either. If I genuinely try to understand the implications of our course of action, but then choose to disregard the very things we're learning, I cannot expect that the people I'm leading will do any differently.

Our words and our actions must remain consistent. That means if what we've attempted doesn't work, then we have to acknowledge our failure, just as much as we would expect those who work with us to acknowledge their own failures.

In some meetings, it really is okay to have what I call the "awkward quiet." Most of us get uncomfortable if at any time a silence of more than a few seconds breaks out. But if we truly want ourselves and those we work with to think clearly about the implications of our actions, then many times it's valuable simply to accept an extended period of quiet and reflection.

A friend and colleague recently wrote to tell me a story that had impressed him so strongly that it still affects him to this day. It also still forms a critical part of his understanding of how to lead. He reminded me that even though I led a large, international organization, I still wanted to know the individuals in various departments, those involved in running the organization. Whenever possible, I asked to attend their planning sessions. I wanted to know more about the individuals who ultimately made our company successful. "You didn't have a 'meet and greet and leave' approach," he said. "You had a 'go and become part of the group' approach."

I did this because as I listened to group discussions over the course of a day or two, ate meals with the participants and chatted over drinks, I discovered a great deal that I would not otherwise have known about our company. At the same time, I was able to encourage the staff and to challenge them to new and greater heights. I didn't want to know only about their professional accomplishments; I wanted to know about their families, about their coworkers and about what they thought the company needed to do to become better.

That's modeling, and to me, it's the only way to go.

Turning around a Classic Fail

Thirty years ago, a "classic fail" almost sank one of the world's biggest corporations. On April 23, 1985, after two years of extensive taste tests and research, the Coca Cola Company replaced its flagship product with what it called New Coke, a concoction that Chairman Roberto C. Goizueta declared, "smoother, rounder yet bolder."

As you may know, the thing promptly bombed.

Around the globe, fans of the old Coke started hoarding their favorite drink. By June, cases of the traditional beverage were selling on the black market for thirty dollars a case, an astronomical price at the time. And less than three months later, on July 11, the company pulled its "smoother, rounder yet bolder" drink from store shelves worldwide.

What went wrong? Despite spending mountains of money on months of expensive taste tests and research, the company had failed to ask the key question: Did fans of the old Coke want a New Coke? "We did not understand the deep emotions of so many of our customers for Coca-Cola," admitted Donald R. Keough, company president. The company had missed the loyalty piece, by light years. In hindsight, it looks as though Coke officials simply assumed that consumers wanted something new, and so they pushed ahead on their conviction—until it turned out to be disastrously wrong.

To their credit, they did an abrupt about-face, hastily reintroducing the old Coke as "Classic Coke." So while they may not have done a great job at the first three I's—inquisitiveness, intentionality, and integration—once they implemented their flawed plan and observed the catastrophic results, they did wonderful (and quick) work at implication. They admitted their mistake, learned a huge lesson about customer loyalty, and made an immediate course correction.

Through the years, the company has continued to try new products (cherry Coke, vanilla Coke, lime Coke, Coke Zero, etc.), but since 1985, it never again failed to ask the key question. And I suppose you could say that Coke has done okay in the intervening decades. In 2014, the company earned a profit of $28 billion dollars on $46 billion dollars of worldwide sales.

Someone I highly respect once told me, "Here's the thing about consequences: They will happen. It is physics. For every action, there is an equal and opposite reaction. That is going to happen, whether or not we pay attention to it. The difference between paying attention to it or not is the difference between implication and ignorance . . . and quite possibly, failure."

But when you do implication right—even if you misfire on some of the other I's—things can still turn out quite well, thank you very much.

The Coil

About a year ago I received a fun email from a friend who could hardly wait to tell me a bit of good news

> Greg,
> Bill forwarded this article today. It never would have happened were it not for YOU.....thank you so much for connecting me with Bill!!!!!
> All is well,
> Larry

I hadn't done much, really. I had independent relationships with both men for years, and one day, I began to think that, perhaps, they should know each other. So with that in mind, I helped to arrange a meeting between them. Several meetings later, they formed a bit of a partnership and I got the satisfaction of knowing something good had happened through my support.

More precisely, it happened through the agency of the Coil.

Through the years, I've watched how the Coil has helped many leaders achieve significant success. In fact, most of those leaders have described the Coil's role as critical to their success. So what is the Coil? Some people think of it as networking, but it's a lot more than that. I've read many good books on networking, with titles such as *Never Eat Alone and Networking Is a Contact Sport,* but the Coil goes far beyond what such books have in mind.

So what is the Coil? It took me a while to get my head around it, but once I did, it radically improved the way I operate. And I think it can do the same for you.

What's a "Coil"?

While I can't remember exactly when I first started thinking of it as "The Coil," I used it to varying degrees long before I named it. Only after naming it, however, did it become the life-enriching, business-enhancing, soul-strengthening force in my life that it is today.

While the Coil is related to networking and the idea that everyone is connected to everyone else through a few personal links, it reaches far beyond both ideas. It's founded on a very simple premise:

> *Recognizing our ability to build on our individual coils allow us to achieve greater results than we otherwise would enjoy.*

It "works," primarily, because it puts in our head a mental image that encourages us to become highly proactive in connecting with others, whoever they may be and whatever they may do. Through these connections come greater opportunities for *everyone* joined in some way to our coil.

The Coil, therefore, is about total connectivity in all aspects of life. It is not merely local, regional, or national in scope, but truly international. It infuses intrigue into life, even when least expected. It's far more than networking and much more than increasing business contacts. At its best, engaging with the Coil becomes a nearly unconscious habit that can bring a surprising richness to everything and everyone it touches.

Why a Coil?

When most people try to create a visual image that represents our personal connections and how our influence spreads, they usually think of the wake of a boat or of the concentric circles produced by a pebble thrown into a pond. Although both of these images provide a sense of how we make connections, they cannot fully illustrate the huge impact of the connectivity of our relationships or of our ability to use those connections in an appropriate way.

I have owned a boat for many years, so I understand that as the boat moves, it leaves behind an ever-widening wake of influence. As the wake gets progressively further away, however, I lose the ability to see how my wake influences someone else (or how their wake influences me). The picture of the wake simply doesn't demonstrate clearly enough for me how one person's influence ends up influencing another, and then a third, and then a fourth. The pebble in thrown in a pond has a similar problem. Yes, we have an expanding circle of influence; but that picture doesn't help me to understand how my relationships interconnect with others and how one individual influences another.

A coil, however, does the trick quite nicely for me.

A coil is a continuous, curving filament, very traceable from its start to its current position. My coil, for example, begins with my birth and tracks my life's twists and turns up to the present day. Your coil follows the same pattern. And when our coils intersect in some way—maybe we have a chance meeting, or someone introduces us, or I attend a function where you're the featured speaker—the relationships and experiences of your coil make some kind of connection with the relationships and experiences of my coil. And what happens next is anyone's guess.

All coils have the potential to intertwine in some way with all other coils. Everybody I ever connect with, somewhere along the line, overlaps with my coil, and sometimes multiple times. The question becomes, then, how and where does my coil intersect with yours? And further, at the point of intersection, for whatever period of time it lasts, how can that connection help me or help you toward the goals we each have in our lives?

I should probably clarify at this point that when I use the word "help," I don't have in mind a single-faceted benefit such as "business networking." That's part of the Coil, of course, but only a part. I've made thousands of helpful business connections through the Coil (this book is an example of one), but a large number of the most fascinating and helpful connections I've made through the Coil have absolutely nothing to do with business or money, and everything to do with enhancing my life in a myriad other ways. Further, the Coil isn't solely about looking for ways to benefit myself; it's also about consciously using my relationships and experiences to benefit others, whether I profit or not.

Perhaps the thing I love best about the Coil is its infinite capacity to surprise. It overflows with serendipity. I never know what gift it will wash up on the shores of my life. It therefore sparks my curiosity, and the more it does, the more I indulge that curiosity. The frequent result? I wind up with all kinds of amazing gifts, things I never could have imagined before I made the Coil a key part of my life. That's serendipity. And I really like it.

Indulge Your Curiosity

When I first started experimenting with the Coil years ago, I had no idea how important it would later become to me. I just set out to have some fun with it. In fact, I often used it to play a little game.

Maybe I was supposed to attend some event where I doubted I would know anyone, or perhaps I walked into an unfamiliar place and wondered if the people there thought I looked as strange to them as they looked to me. So I started playing *I Wonder If*. As in, "I wonder if there's anyone here I might know, or if we might know someone in common?" At first, I thought, *There's no way.* But I chose to play the game, just to see for sure.

Very quickly, it became an incredibly fascinating exercise. I told my wife about the game, but she just kind of rolled her eyes. I'll never forget the time she and I went to a big dinner in downtown L.A., sponsored by Northern Trust Bank. I said to her, "I don't think we'll know anybody here. I don't expect to know anybody here, other than bank staff, so they don't count. I want to see how long it takes for us, just by mingling during the cocktail hour, before we find someone who knows somebody we know."

As we walked into the main room, the first couple we met looked maybe ten years older than I am. I approached the man and said, "Hi, how are you? I'm Greg. Are you from this area?"

"No," he replied. "We're from Florida."

His wife had been listening and quickly joined the conversation. "Yes, we're from Florida," she said, "but we also have a place in Grand Rapids."

Immediately, my antenna went up. I had nabbed my first clue that I might find a mutual connection here, as unlikely as it might seem. I couldn't think of a significant tie to Florida, but I did have one in Grand Rapids, Michigan. So I took a chance by asking an off-the-wall question, one of the keys to tapping into the power of the Coil.

"Well, I'm sure you don't know him," I replied, giving them an out, "but my college roommate and best friend—we were in each other's wedding—has a small business in Grand Rapids. His name is Tom Dykstra."

Immediately the man's face lit up. "Oh, Tom!" he said. "We've known Tom forever. We knew Tom's dad, and they banked with us for years." I soon found out the couple owned a community bank in Grand Rapids. And I thought, *We haven't been into this game for even five minutes, and already I've made a significant connection.*

That encounter really encouraged me to play the game more often; I think it even impressed my wife. I continued to play the game repeatedly over the next few weeks, and similar things kept happening, over and over again. One night I accompanied my wife to an art festival in our home town, and as I sat on a bench reading, I occasionally looked up to watch people go by. I remember thinking, *Is somebody going to go by tonight that I recognize? And if I do recognize someone, what will I do about it?*

Not long afterwards, I spotted a couple walk on by whom I hadn't seen since the mid-90s. I recognized him as the former CEO of Coldwell Banker. He hadn't noticed me, and I decided to get up and walk over to him from behind. "Hey Joe," I said, "how are you? Good to see you."

We had a short conversation, and eventually he even signed my wife's visitor's book and gave her his email to receive more information about her artwork. We had a nice time chatting, and that was it.

I could have let Joe just pass by; after all, I didn't know him well. I hadn't seen him in ages. I had no particular agenda in mind, other than playing the game. I wasn't looking for business and I didn't need to refresh an old professional connection. But by this time, the Coil already had taught me that connecting itself is The Thing. A big part of the fun (and the benefit) comes in the amazing surprises you inevitably get by taking the risk to attempt a connection.

Expect to Be Surprised

The Coil generates surprises in all sorts of ways. Sometimes, you make an unexpected connection that provides a key to furthering one of your business interests. At other times, you meet someone who can't enhance your business in any way, but who has a story so fascinating that you'll never forget it. And at still other times, the Coil serves as the fountainhead for beginning a brand new phase in life.

In my work as a consultant, I've helped any number of people who have desired to make a fresh start in life, but who have come to me convinced that they didn't know *anybody*. Before I began this phase of my career, I'd never realized how many individuals, all of them with prodigious talents and wide influence, really, truly believe that they have no relationships and *no* connections outside of some very narrow field. And if they want to get out of that field, many of them often come to our first meeting almost in despair.

But the Coil tells me that every one of them knows far more individuals than they think they do.

One enormously impressive man came to me after spending his entire career in a single organization. He had oversight of literally thousands of people. He wasn't ready to retire, but he'd risen as far as he thought he could in the organization and he'd concluded that the time had come for him to shift gears and find another place of service. But he didn't know where to begin.

"I don't know who I even know outside of my old world, Greg," he told me. "Where will I start? I've always been where I am."

"Well," I said, "let's talk about your coil."

"What's a coil?" he asked.

"It's all the people you know who you don't normally think about, individuals whom you really do know," I replied. "There are people in your coil with whom you can connect." He clearly didn't seem to share my confidence, but he said he'd give it a try.

Just a few days later, he called back. He'd compiled a full page of names. His list not only surprised him, it staggered him. He had no idea. On his list appeared all kinds of CEOs and major executives, along with one U.S. Senator. "Oh, yeah," he said, "she called me her favorite. And she said that if I ever wanted to call her, here was her number."

"Okay," I answered, "so you don't know *anybody?* Now that we've covered that territory, what are we going to do, now that we know somebody?" We then discussed how he could appropriately use the individuals in his coil to make some inquiries about possible next steps for him. And what happened then, I've seen happen innumerable times. As he contacted different individuals in his coil, they often introduced him to others in their coils. One overlap led to another, and in a very short while, he found a perfect position for himself, outside of his old field. Today, he's thriving and happy. We still talk occasionally on the phone, and it tickles me to hear about his exciting new adventures.

One of my friends laughingly says, "Greg, you're only one percent removed from anybody. No matter where we go, you seem either to know somebody or you're talking about somebody that the two of you know in common."

Actually, I'm convinced that any leader can enjoy that kind of connectivity, to one degree or another. My coil may seem larger than my friend's, but only because some of us have been around longer and worked in more places than others. My friend's comment, however, brings up another difference between how the Coil operates and how networking typically works.

I've mentioned already how networking tends to focus exclusively on business contacts, while engaging with the Coil may take a person on all kinds of surprising excursions, some related to business and many not even remotely connected to business. Networking, therefore, by its very nature, concentrates on growing *itself.* In the old days, it was all about increasing the size of your Rolodex. Today, it's all about making hundreds of connections on Linked In® or maxing out your cell phone's memory with the contact information of potential business associates. But the power of the Coil doesn't limit itself to the size of your own individual coil.

The Coil really flexes its muscle as one person's coil overlaps with another's—and it "works" because *it's based on genuine relationship, not merely having a phone number or email.* With traditional networking, you make a call and that's it. With the Coil, you make a connection and then watch as all sorts of other connections get made as one individual's coil overlaps with another, and then another, and then another. In many ways, it's the difference between addition and multiplication.

Be Deliberate

As you might guess, the Coil works best when you engage with it proactively. You have to be willing to speak to people you don't know, to introduce yourself and risk an actual conversation, the contours of which you can't know ahead of time. That's the key to the whole enterprise.

When I first introduced one client to the Coil, he expressed extreme skepticism about the value of the idea. But as he started using it, he saw its power go to work for him. At the beginning, he sometimes felt shocked that individuals he didn't yet know well would even want to talk to him (although it really shouldn't have come as a shock, since he's widely known and most people like it when "celebrities" want to connect). But then, as he started to become more aware of his own coil and how it worked, he started paying more attention to his environment—the books in someone's library, the kind of car an acquaintance drove, the tone of voice somebody used, who was in his vicinity that day and how they might share some connection. The more he picked up on these clues, and the more he intentionally started asking appropriate questions based on those clues, the more his coil expanded and the more interesting connections he started making. Many of those connections gave his business a boost. But many more simply made his life richer, fuller, more interesting.

What I call "Coil stories" happen all the time, and they can happen in an instant. But they happen much more frequently and in more interesting and surprising ways when you get very intentional about interacting with your coil. That intentionality has at least five parts to it.

1. *Observe and listen*

   Get your antennae up. Observe what's around you. Note tone of voice, facial expressions, body language. Listen carefully for clues that might tell you something important about a person or group. Take a keen interest in your environment and know what and who is in it. Be outward-focused rather than inward-focused. Indulge your curiosity—if something piques your interest, discover what you can about it. Engage your sense of wonder and enjoy being a learner. Find out "stuff," just because it's fun.

2. *Ask appropriate, clarifying questions*

When you hear or see something that interests you, express your interest by asking good questions about it. "I find that fascinating," you say. "Could you tell me more?" or "I'm sure you don't know this person, but . . . ." or "Help me to understand . . . ." or "I'm just curious . . . ." or "I was just wondering . . . ." I stress "appropriate" questions, because there is a way to ask questions that sounds offensive, irritating, or even scary. Most people, however, love talking about themselves, so when you truly want to learn about them—and you don't give the impression you're asking only because you want something from them—they're typically more than willing to expound.

3. *Think of possible connecting points*

As you observe, listen, and ask appropriate questions, deliberately ransack your brain to see if you can identify any possible point of contact between the individual and you. Maybe you share a taste for '57 Chevys. Maybe you both visited Disneyland recently. Maybe you hail from the same state, or attended the same school, or enjoy similar kinds of music. Whatever the connection might be, keep it in mind until the right time comes to . . .

4. *Take a risk and ask "off the wall" questions*

One of my favorite questions, as you've seen, is some version of, "You probably don't know this person, but by any chance, have you ever met fill in the blank?" Very often, the individual has never heard of your friend or acquaintance. But you'd be surprised at how frequently their eyes light up and they reply in a delighted, animated voice, "Why, yes! In fact, my sister-in-law used to babysit him years ago, back in Minnesota!" (Don't laugh, because that one actually happened to me.)

5. *Look to give as much as you get*

Never forget that the Coil is all about relationships. It "works" because you and I take a genuine interest in the individuals we meet, beyond anything they might be able to do for us. In fact, the greatest pleasure I get from the Coil these days is not what I get through it, but what it enables me to give to others. I take great delight in trying to figure out how I might be able to help *Jim* accomplish X by meeting *Bob*. Similarly, I greatly enjoy the intellectual puzzle of trying to understand how some insight I gained over here might relate to another insight gained over there, and how the combination of the two might be able to help an acquaintance overcome some challenge that I heard about through the Coil.

But none of these wonderful things (or at least, far fewer of them) happen unless I deliberately choose to engage with the Coil. Intentionality makes all the difference.

Make It a Habit

The easiest way to deliberately engage with the Coil is to make it a habit. When it starts to become something you just naturally do, wherever you are, that's when the real fun begins.

Some time ago I was asked to speak at the University of California-Irvine in regard to some of the very topics addressed in this book. I began explaining how we connect with others by learning to be empathetic toward them. "Sometimes," I said, "it can be appropriate to just slightly touch somebody's shoulder or elbow. But it has to be appropriate."

As I spoke, I touched, very lightly on the left shoulder, an African American woman sitting nearby. Normally when I do this, I sense the person relaxing; but this time, I sensed exactly the opposite. Her whole body seemed to tense up. When I noticed what had happened, I turned to her and asked, "Can you tell me what just happened? What was your experience, just now? What went on for you?" She returned my gaze as forty other individuals looked at us, all of them international scholars and people of color, leaders of the school's new class of doctoral students.

"I'm a black woman," she replied tersely. "You're a white man. And you've just invaded my space."

At that moment, I had several choices. I could say, "Oh, that's scary. I'm so sorry." And I could have walked away and tried to move on to some other topic. But I chose to stay and enter into a conversation with her. Why? That's become my habit. It's part of how I regularly and deliberately engage with the Coil.

In very short order, we ended up having a fascinating discussion about what it feels like as a black woman to have your space invaded by a white man. And it wasn't a discussion between just the two of us. The whole room joined us and we all gained the kind of insights you acquire only through a genuine and unplanned conversation.

"You all come from different perspectives," I said at one point. "Do you tend to invite people into your space, or do you usually put them out?" We discussed the question for several minutes, trading ideas about personal space, empathy, and building relationships.

Once the meeting ended, a fair number of students came up to ask questions or to just talk. One of those individuals was this delightful black woman. She greeted me with a big smile and gave me a wonderful, warm hug. She also asked for my card. It felt to me like a terrific capstone to a very good day.

But it turned out that wasn't the end of it—with the Coil, it hardly ever is. My habit of choosing to engage with the Coil on that day and in that way led to another student's choice a few days later to call me. We had another productive discussion and at the end of our conversation, we left the door wide open for further engagement.

Now, imagine what *might* have taken place had I never made the Coil a part of the way I typically operate. When she told me, quite honestly, "I'm a black woman, you're a white man, and you've just violated my space," how do you think I would have responded, apart from my habit of engaging with the Coil? By nature, I'm an introvert, not an extrovert. I don't like conflict of any kind. I hate making people feel uncomfortable. So I have little doubt that her words and tone of voice would have sent me scurrying away, and I would have escaped from that room just as fast as I could have managed it. There would have been no discussion. There would have been no learning. There would have been no smile and no warm hug.

In fact, I'm pretty sure there would have been just one offended black woman and one very skittish white man.

When we habitually engage with the coil, in a sense, we *appropriately* enter into somebody else's space. So when we get rebuffed, do we let fear scare us away? Or do we try to hang in there and see what caused the rejection? Or when someone wants to enter our space, again in an appropriate way, do we rebuff them? Or do we fully engage with them through the Coil to see where it all might lead?

Remember, the Coil isn't only about reaching out. It's also about being available. The networking books I've read tend to describe what we need to do to reach out. But the Coil is all about interrelationships, about how my coil and your coil overlap, for the benefit of everyone involved.

Accept, Don't Demand

Although everyone can benefit from the Coil, Type A personalities often take a while to really "get" how it works best. There's a perfectly good reason why this should be so. Type A's like to take charge, get things done, waste no time. They're exceptionally focused on some specific task (or tasks) they want to accomplish.

Meanwhile, the Coil just yawns.

The Coil, you see, is all about human relationships, and human relationships tend to evolve in unpredictable, haphazard, and unfocused ways. You can't go to the Coil, demanding that it give you only what you want. You can't order it to enrich you every Thursday at 7:15 a.m. sharp. The Coil is more like a lazy river than a lap pool, more like a Sunday afternoon stroll through Central Park than a 10K run through Manhattan. You can't predict what will come to you through the Coil, and you can't demand that it bring you this or that and only this or that.

What you can do is to learn to appreciate and accept whatever it delivers, valuing those gifts as the unexpected surprises that they really are.

Sometimes, the Coil brings you a gift that makes a tremendous difference to your business and career. Sometimes, it blesses you with an amazing insight that stays with you for days, weeks, even years. Sometimes, it introduces you to a new friend, or reintroduces you to an old friend. Sometimes, it brings back a long-ago memory, or gives you an idea for a book, or creates a thirst for a fresh experience. And sometimes, frankly, it's hard to tell exactly what it brings.

Always, though, you can expect it to generate a fun, new story. Tons of those, actually.

A client once asked my wife and me to attend a professional boxing match, held as a fundraising event for some charity. We went because my client made it clear he really wanted us there. "Come early," he told me, "because my friend, who's the promoter of the fight, said he'll take us beforehand to meet the fighters in the locker room."

"Okay," I said. Now, I'm not much of a boxing fan, but I do love something different. And this was certainly something different. So, of course, we agreed to go.

Once we arrived, I started talking to the guy who managed one of the evening's main fighters. The others in my group started wandering off, just to look around. After they jawed with each other for a while, they started leaving. "Come on, Greg," they yelled, "we have to go!"

My client gave me a look as if to say, "Okay, just how many people do you and that guy know in common?" I hadn't met the fight manager before that night, but I had learned a lot about him. I learned why he does what he does. I learned where his fighter was from and where else the man fought. I learned the location of their gym. Those things felt far more interesting and satisfying to me than a tour of the locker room. And the manager quite simply intrigued me. While he seemed weirdly dressed, I learned he had a thriving business, with fighters all over the Santa Monica area coming to him to get trained.

I didn't obtain anything that night that put money in my wallet. I didn't make any connections that resulted in new consulting work. But I did gain a fascinating few nuggets about an exotic world I had hardly imagined, and that evening my coil grew. I now have a contact in the boxing world, if I ever need it. I don't know that I ever will, but it's there. And that one contact could lead me to any number of other fascinating people and places and ideas and experiences.

What happened that evening many years ago reminds me why I love the Coil. Once you stop telling it what it has to bring you, and start accepting whatever it plops at your doorstep, you notice your life being enriched in ways you simply never could have imagined.

Try It, You'll Like It

I said at the beginning of this chapter that the Coil has helped many leaders I know to achieve significant success, and that many of them have told me it's become a critical part of whatever achievements they've amassed. That's all true.

It's also true that the Coil enriches lives in countless ways that have nothing to do with business, professional success, or making money. It has given me moments of startling beauty, experiences of profound meaning, and lots and lots and lots of silly, inconsequential, but fun times that would have come to me in no other way.

That's all true, and that's all good. But for you, in many ways, it's also largely irrelevant. Because the real point of this chapter is not to talk about my experiences with the Coil, but to encourage you to have your own experiences on your own coil.

So indulge me for a moment and think about your coil. What is it like?

"I don't have one," you say.

Pardon me, but yes, you do. And it's larger than you imagine. So start thinking about it right now, outside of your usual routine. As you experience life and as you intentionally try to link your coil with the coils of all sorts of interesting people, see how quickly you can make new connections.

If it helps, make a game out of it. Don't put any unnecessary pressure on yourself. Observe what's going around you, listen for clues, and then start asking questions: "You probably don't know so and so, but..." Remember, you have to ask the question. You must be prepared to risk moving into that unfamiliar space—appropriately, of course, but deliberately choosing to move into it.

Regardless of where we are and where we go and what we do, we all have the ability to take appropriate advantage of every opportunity and conversation that presents itself to us. We all can begin to explore a wonderful, exotic, fresh new world that we've yet to visit. While it's not always easy, nearly always it's rewarding. The question becomes, do we really want to be a leader? Do we genuinely want to get connected to a broader world that gives us the opportunity to gain an expanding base of knowledge and relationships?

The most successful leaders I know all have inquiring minds. Many of them even think of themselves as philosophers. They are certainly curious about how things work and how they might work better. Those with a burning desire to "get to the top" constantly search for more knowledge about their job, their organization, and their industry. They enjoy and want to be part of the team, but they also have a driving desire to lead the team.

If you see yourself anywhere in this description, then I commend to you the Coil. Try it, you'll like it. You'll especially like the wide variety of gifts it brings to you, surprising gifts that will enrich your world and make you a better person . . . even as they do the same for those connected to you.

Who's Your Mentor?

Are you a leader? If so, do you feel lonely?

Whether anyone likes it or not, the feeling of being alone is simply part of the calling to leadership. I've yet to find a senior leader who, at his or her most honest, didn't acknowledge (and sometimes lament) the loneliness factor.

Why do leaders often feel so lonely? For one thing, we have few people with whom we can share the load we bear. We can't alarm coworkers or investors by revealing sensitive information. We must avoid giving ammunition to our competitors by exposing company weaknesses. We have to keep company secrets under wraps to give important initiatives the best chance at success. Consequently, we have to keep our mouths shut when it might feel better to talk. Loneliness is part of the job description.

I rarely felt threatened when people challenged me in some aspect of my leadership, but I often felt alone, because like every other executive. I wondered, *Who is here with me? Who's here to support me?* It didn't feel as though anyone truly had my back.

But everyone needs to know that *someone* has their back. So what's a leader to do?

Get the Support You Need

In one way or another, you need to find those with whom you can safely and helpfully interact. But *how* can you find other executives who serve, or have served, in positions similar to your own? How can you forge the kind of professional relationships that will take the edge off of the inevitable loneliness that every executive feels? With whom can you have beneficial conversations that encourage and challenge you, peer-to-peer interactions that help you to reach your stated goals—all in a safe and uplifting environment?

I strongly recommend that you seek out a coach or mentor. Find someone with whom you can truly connect, a person of experience and wisdom who can validate your perspective as well as challenge and/or affirm your intended course of action. A coach or mentor can often provide exactly the kind of assistance and support that most leaders long for and require.

A few years ago, an accomplished surgeon asked in a *New Yorker* article, "Top Athletes and Singers Have Coaches, Should You?"[3] He described how he consistently bested national averages in regard to his surgical rates of complications—until one year, he didn't. How could he regain his edge? "It started to seem that the only direction things could go from here was the wrong one," he wrote. Although he had enjoyed great success for many years, he eventually stopped making progress. He'd gotten stuck. His performance had ceased to improve and seemed in real danger of deteriorating.

The good news is that this leader recognized his problem and began to look for an answer. He needed someone who could help him see the implications of his choices and how to rethink his usual operating procedures so he could start improving again. "Getting better at what you do is about taking areas of your un-

---

3   Atul Gawande, "Personal Best: Top Athletes and Singers Have Coaches, Should You?" *The New Yorker*, October 3, 2011.

conscious incompetence and making it more conscious to your-self," he wrote. "Whether it's a sport or anything else, take it into its component parts." This man, and many like him, have found a coach or mentor to be invaluable.

A Personal Endorsement

As a former athlete myself, for decades I've understood the value of coaching. Not only was I coached, but for many years, I also coached other athletes, helping them to become more success-ful in the technical aspects of their sports. That's one reason why, even today, I enthusiastically endorse the idea that we all need a coach or mentor with the ability to help us become all that we can be, in the most holistic way possible.

Harvey Chrouser served for many years as the athletic direc-tor at Wheaton College. In 1951, he founded Honey Rock camp in Northern Wisconsin, the college's outdoor center for leader-ship development. During two summers at Honey Rock, he and I spent countless hours together as he helped me to better un-derstand how to lead and direct people. I can't say he was always an easy taskmaster, but he willingly spent a vast amount of time with me. Over countless hours we discussed why he had decided to start a program that so creatively challenged people to go be-yond themselves.

Don Church, an outstanding coach, probably influenced me in my leadership ideals more than any other individual. Eventu-ally he became a very close personal friend. As I watched him intentionally do whatever he could to help others become the best possible version of themselves, his perspective and coach-ing habits began to infuse my own life. In many discussions with Don over the years, I started rethinking my whole conception of what it meant to be a servant leader, and in the process, what it might look like to encourage and coach or mentor others. He's really the one responsible for prompting me to choose a journey focused on doing whatever I could do to help others become all that they could be.

The Many Faces of Coaching and Mentoring

A lot of coaching and mentoring is about helping people to face into their realities, as my good friends, Drs. Henry Cloud and John Townsend, would say. Those realities can be both very pleasant and not pleasant at all. A good coach or mentor can encourage us to engage with our unpleasant realities as well as the pleasant ones.

I currently mentor a man born several decades ago in Afghanistan. As a young boy, Alex immigrated to the United States with his father and slightly older brother. During the Soviet occupation of Afghanistan, his father took his sons on a dangerous trip over the mountains into Pakistan. At one point, a bullet grazed Alex's left eyebrow; moments later, he watched his father kill a Soviet soldier.

After the trio arrived in the United States, it became too difficult for Alex's father to care for him and a loving Texas family adopted him. To this day, Alex does not know his exact birthday or even the year of his birth. He's not certain of how many siblings he has or anything about his mother.

As part of helping Alex with his businesses, I've tried to help him face into his realities. Those realities, of course, are far greater than just his business issues. He sometimes wakes up shaking in the middle of the night, looks in the mirror, and sees the scar left so long ago by a bullet meant for his head. I try to help him integrate that frightening part of his life with his wonderful experience of being adopted and loved by an American family, as well as integrating his professional success. But he still knows there's "something missing." As a coach, I can help him prime his business for growth by helping him to understand some of the other needs in his life.

Others recognize their need for a coach because they understand they sometimes need a nudge. One of the CEOs I work with has told me more than once, "I need you to push me occasionally." In his case, part of my responsibility is to understand when he's starting to coast. As I become aware of it, I help bring him back to focus on the larger responsibilities that he and his organization face. I do this by intentionally asking questions that target the relevant issue.

My primary task with other leaders is to help them become aware of how they're spending their time. Periodically, therefore, we conduct time audits. The idea of time audits came from my work with Henry Cloud, who described our work together in a chapter called "The Audit" in his book, The One Life Solution. We often don't recognize how unproductive our schedules have really become. A time audit can speak volumes.

One of my fairly recent coaching clients inherited an established family business. The company has done quite well historically, but in the last few years it began losing traction to competitors. In this case, my coaching has focused on helping the owner see the need to get ahead of the curve by better anticipating customers' needs and the changing competition. He is coming to recognize the danger of failing to adequately consider the shifting dynamics of his market. By asking a lot of clarifying questions, I've helped him to better understand what impacts him, his customers, and his potential clients.

Another coaching client works in the educational field, which has required me to adapt my approach to the unique needs of a non-private sector organization. This client needs to remember his personal strengths and weaknesses and how his personality fits within the constructs of his organization. In addition, he must be able to clearly articulate his employees' need to grow and change in a way that's very difficult to manage, lead and coach. In this case, I've begun to broach the idea of the significant difference between false *bravado* confidence and *authentic* confidence.

Yet another coaching client controlled the majority of his market for a significant time. As the years have gone by, however, many competitors have begun to challenge that control. Our discussions have centered on effectively responding to the market, anticipating its direction, and analyzing its origin. We've also talked about two key employees who appear to be heading in opposite directions. One of them has shown a growing interest in making a difference for the company by bringing creative solutions to the executive team. His supervisor, however, wants the company to continue doing what it's always done and has discouraged any ideas that might require change, even if they hold out the promise of new growth. My client doesn't want to lose either employee—so as the leader, how should he respond to this difficult workplace dynamic? A coach/mentor can ask the right kind of questions to help a client make the decisions best suited for his or her organization.

Harvard Weighs In

An insightful article in the *Harvard Business Review* recently reported the results of a two-year study that looked into "the type of advice top executives require and how they get it."[4] The authors researched how CEOs of large organizations acquire the "seasoned counsel and feedback" they need to serve as effective leaders.

Of forty-five CEOs who had formal mentoring arrangements, 84 percent said their mentors had helped them avoid costly mistakes and more quickly become proficient in their roles. Another 76 percent said they better fulfilled stakeholder expectations; 71 percent reported company performance had improved; and 69 percent said they were making better decisions. Gavin Patterson, CEO of BT Group, summed up the value of mentoring by calling it "a more practical way to develop."

The article compares mentoring to an apprenticeship, where

---

4   Suzanne Janasz and Maury Peiperl, "Managing Yourself: CEOs Need Mentors Too." *Harvard Business Review*, April 2015, 100-103.

the mentee first observes the expert, then executes tasks while being supervised, then over time gains crucial knowledge, and finally masters the role. Since most CEOs can't be away from their jobs for long periods, formal school settings usually do not provide a viable option for acquiring the insight they need. Mentors often provide a good resource to help them sharpen their thinking and give them understanding into decisions they must make on issues they've not yet encountered.

So what's the difference between mentoring and coaching? While executive coaches usually provide great feedback and help clients improve their managerial skills, most of them have never worked in roles comparable to those of the CEOs they coach. "Mentors, by contrast," the article declares, "are role models who have 'been there and done that.' They offer timely, context-specific counsel drawn from experience." They have great wisdom to offer, along with extensive networks built over decades.

So if one mentor is good, can two be better? The answer is often "yes." One CEO declared, "The two-mentor model is the ideal model. If offered twice the time with one of them, I wouldn't swap."[5]

The article highlights three characteristics that effective mentors must have: (1) Experience relevant to the CEO; (2) A broad perspective; (3) The ability to foster an environment of trust. Discussions between mentors and mentees must remain confidential. "Only a certain level of issues can be raised with an internal mentor," explained Peter Lynas, CFO of BAE Systems, while Robert Carr, chairman of BAE Systems, emphasized the importance of "being able to talk to someone in confidence who is not a stakeholder or a paymaster."[6]

---

5   Ibid, 101.

6   Ibid., 102.

Effective mentors typically have ten to fifteen more years of experience than the CEO mentee, which often means they're semi-retired and serving on multiple boards.

Storytelling, the article says, plays a significant and sometimes even crucial role in the mentor/mentee relationship, an assertion I find to be both fascinating and true. Stories can effectively transmit valuable advice based on "real life" experience, and since they elicit emotion and reflect empathy, they also tend to stick longer in memory. In addition, they imply lessons without explicitly stating them, and since they're about someone else, they're "psychologically safe." Stories often prompt the mentee to wonder, "What would I do in the same situation?" Finally, stories often prompt the mentee to believe that, just as the mentor succeeded, so can he or she. That leads naturally to an increase in confidence that in itself paves the way for success.

A Basic Template

I am a firm believer in a three-part coaching/mentoring methodology:

- Affirm
- Challenge
- Affirm again.

At the very least, I want my coaching clients to feel encouraged and affirmed as they leave our times together—but at the same time, I want them to feel challenged in some specific way to become better. And I always strive to pair that challenge with a commitment to follow up within a certain amount of time, an effective strategy that provides the sort of accountability that leads to action.

Although I have an interest in a client's temperament and want to help the individual to become more balanced in his or her personality traits, I always try to bring our conversations back to content. What is the leader going to *do*? In my view, we must deal with the things that prevent improvement and growth due to something substantive taking place in the leader's life. While this may include considerations of personal temperament, I focus primarily on content, on substance—on developing and implementing a clearly defined action step that directly addresses one or more key issues of growth.

It often helps in these cases to invoke The 24 Hour Rule. Very few things need immediate response. But by thinking over a significant problem for a full day, you take the stress level down and allow yourself to properly reflect on, not obsess over, the critical issue in front of you.

Still Learning

The good news for me is that I keep learning, growing and assisting others. Just today I had lunch with one of my own mentors. We discussed how I'm spending my time, what I'm doing, how I'm trying to balance my life, and how I could become even better at what I do. He always challenges my thinking, but he also always affirms me. I know he's for me and he'll always be there for me.

But do you know the curious thing? Over the last few years, I've also become one of his mentors. Although he mentors me, I also mentor him. We have found that both of us have areas in life where we can benefit from a coach/mentor, and both of us have life experiences that we can tap to coach and mentor the other.

Frankly, I love the two-way street. I love the journey. And I especially love that it leads to so many fascinating destinations.

Made in the USA
San Bernardino, CA
23 December 2016